to Mary & Gary,

May you know the
love that satisfies!

Christopher Wit

THE LOVE THAT SATISFIES

reflections on eros & agape

CHRISTOPHER WEST

ASCENSION PRESS

West Chester, Pennsylvania

Nihil obstat: Rev. Robert A. Pesarchick, S.T.D.
                         Censor Librorum
                         June 20, 2007

Imprimatur: +Justin Cardinal Rigali
                         Archbishop of Philadelphia
                         June 21, 2007

Ascension Press
Post Office Box 1990
West Chester, PA 19380
Orders: 1-800-376-0520
www.AscensionPress.com

Cover design: The Design Works Group, Inc., Sisters, Oregon

Printed in the United States of America
07 08 09 10 11 7 6 5 4 3 2

ISBN: 978-1-934217-13-9

To Father Jim Otto, whose
spiritual guidance has been invaluable.

CONTENTS

ABBREVIATIONS

BMA *Bono in Conversation with Michka Assayas* (Riverhead Books, 2005).
BNA *Be Not Afraid*, Andre Frossard and John Paul II (Image Books, 2005)
CCC *Catechism of the Catholic Church* (Libreria Editrice Vaticana, 1997)
CS *Closing Speeches*, Vatican Council II (Pauline, 1965)
CTH *Crossing the Threshold of Hope*, John Paul II (Knopf, 1994)
DV *Dominum et Vivificantem*, John Paul II's Encyclical Letter on the Holy Spirit (Pauline, 1986)
EKH *Everything You Ever Wanted to Know about Heaven*, Peter Kreeft (Ignatius Press, 1990)
FC *Familiaris Consortio*, John Paul II's Apostolic Exhortation on the Role of the Christian Family in the Modern World (Pauline, 1981)
FR *Fides et Ratio*, John Paul II's Encyclical on Faith and Reason (Pauline, 1998)
GN *Good News About Sex & Marriage: Answers to Your Honest Questions About Catholic Teaching*, Revised Edition, Christopher West (Servant, 2004)
GS *Gaudium et Spes*, Vatican II's Pastoral Constitution on the Church in the Modern World (Pauline, 1965)
HCW *How to Win the Culture War*, Peter Kreeft (InterVarsity Press, 2002)
KW *Karol Wojtyla: The Thought of the Man Who Became Pope John Paul II*, Rocco Buttiglione (Eerdmans, 1997).
LF *Letter to Families*, John Paul II's Letter to Families in the Year of the Family (Pauline, 1994)
LR *Love and Responsibility*, Karol Wojtyla's philosophical work on human sexuality (Ignatius Press, 1981)
MD *Mulieris Dignitatem*, John Paul II's Apostolic Letter on the Dignity and Vocation of Women (Pauline, 1988)
MI *Memory and Identity*, John Paul II (Rizzoli, 2005)
NM *The Nuptial Mystery*, Angelo Cardinal Scola (Eerdmans, 2005)
NMI *Novo Millennio Ineunte*, John Paul II's Apostolic Letter at the Close of the Great Jubilee (Pauline, 2001)
OL *Orientale Lumen*, John Paul II's Apostolic Letter on the Light of the East (Pauline, 1995)
RH *Redemptor Hominis*, John Paul II's Encyclical Letter on the Redeemer of Man (Pauline, 1979)
TBB *Theology of the Body for Beginners*, Christopher West (Ascension Press, 2004)
TBE *Theology of the Body Explained*, Christopher West (Pauline, 2003)
TJ *Tract on 1 John*, Saint Augustine
TOB *Man and Woman He Created Them: A Theology of the Body*, John Paul II's general audience addresses on Human Love in the Divine Plan (Pauline, 2006)
VS *Veritatis Splendor*, John Paul II's Encyclical Letter on the Splendor of Truth (Pauline, 2003)

Acknowledgments

My thanks to the following men and women who helped me with this book:

Melanie Anderson, Jeanette Clark, Angelique Cummings, Gary Cummings, Bill Donaghy, Brian Gail, Brother Gregory, Meghann Harden, Robin Hatley, Lisa Lickona, Steve Motyl, Matthew Pinto, Lorraine Ranalli, Claudia Roebuck, Maureen Snook, Rose Sweet, Soren West, Jay Wonacott, and Katrina Zeno.

The staff of Ascension Press, who were a pleasure to work with as always.

The prayers and support of my wife, Wendy, and my four children, John Paul, Thomas, Beth, and Isaac, were invaluable.

INTRODUCTION

N ot long ago I was pushing the "seek" button on my car radio looking for a decent song. Station 1: "Love me, love me, say that you love me." Station 2: "I'm keeping you forever and for always, we will be together all of our days." Station 3: "When a man loves a woman..." As Paul McCartney put it, "You think that people woulda had enough of silly love songs. I look around me and I see it isn't so, oh no."

And, yet, in the midst of so many songs celebrating love, there is also plenty of angst coming through the airwaves. I'm dating myself here, but do you remember Gloria Gaynor's feminist anthem from the '70s? "Go on now go! Walk out the door! Just turn around now, 'cause you're not welcome anymore." It took a decade, but men eventually fired back with an anthem of their own from Bon Jovi: "Shot through the heart, and you're to blame. You give love a bad name."

So, are we to agree with the Beatles that "All You Need Is Love" or with the J. Geils Band that "Love Stinks"? That would depend, of course, on what we mean by that slippery four-letter word, *love*. In this book, we will turn to the wisdom of both Pope Benedict XVI and John Paul II in order to shed some much-needed light on the issue of love. Pope Benedict writes,

> Today, the term "love" has become one of the most frequently used and misused of words, a word to which we attach quite different meaning…We speak of love of country, love of one's profession, love between friends, love of work, love between parents and children, love between family members, love of neighbor and love of God. Amid this multiplicity of meanings, however, one in particular stands out: love between man and woman, where body and soul are inseparably joined and human beings glimpse an apparently irresistible promise of happiness. This would seem to be the very epitome of love; all other kinds of love immediately seem to fade in comparison (*God Is Love*, n. 2).

This book focuses on this last kind of love—the love that promises such happiness but so often leads to despair; the love that seems to be the epitome of all love but which relatively few people find in a measure that satisfies. Why should this be the case? Why is the love between man and woman so attractive and illusive, demanding and rewarding, restrictive and liberating, painful and ecstatic, messy and beautiful, maddening and fulfilling? Our world is saturated with sex but remains starved for love. Why? Perhaps, as Waylon Jennings put it, we're "lookin' for love in all the wrong places, lookin' for love in too many faces." Where, then, is the right place and whose, then, is the right face in which to look for love?

By reflecting on key passages from Pope Benedict's grand encyclical *God Is Love (Deus Caritas Est)*, this book explores these and many other questions with the goal of pointing all who read it toward the love that satisfies.

God Is Love

Encyclical letters are one of the most important teaching platforms of a pope. They express the pope's mind on what he personally considers to be a matter of great importance for the Church and humanity. A pope's *first* encyclical does this all the more so, offering an important window into the tone and direction of his pontificate.

Many Vatican observers expected "God's Rottweiler"—a nickname the pope got from his previous job safeguarding Church doctrine in the Congregation for the Doctrine of the Faith—to use his first encyclical to bark at wayward theologians and crack down on matters of Church discipline. Instead, Pope Benedict "wanted here—at the beginning of [his] Pontificate—to clarify some essential facts concerning the love which God mysteriously and gratuitously offers man, together with the intrinsic link between that Love and the reality of human love" (n. I). Those who give the pope's message the attention it deserves will discover that the Catholic Church—despite all the supposed anti-sex sentiment—has a vision of sexual love far more glorious than anything Sigmund Freud, Hugh Hefner, Britney Spears, or Howard Stern could dream of or imagine. It seems, however, that few people have given this encyclical the attention it deserves. This book aims to help remedy that, exposing the riches of the pope's unmined treasure to an audience that might not be inclined to pick up a papal document or may find it difficult to digest on its own.

One might ask, with all the other pressing issues in the world—unrest in the Middle East, growing tensions between Muslims and Christians, terrorism, war, famine, poverty, AIDS—why the Vicar of Christ would choose to discuss the love between man and woman in his first encyclical? Those who want to see in the pope's letter yet another example of the Church's harping on the "pelvic issues" while ignoring the more important things in life will miss altogether the wisdom at work here. This wisdom seeks to heal the world's ills by going to the root of all the world's problems: lack of love and, more specifically, lack of love between man and woman. Man has turned his back on the God who *is* love. This has had disastrous consequences for human relationships, beginning with the relationship of man and woman. Only by returning to the God who is love can men and women learn to love one another rightly. Much is at stake, for the love between the sexes is the foundation stone of human life and the building block of civilization.

One would be hard pressed to find any societal problem that cannot be traced to a breakdown of this most fundamental human relationship. The outline of Benedict's encyclical seems to demonstrate the point that a just social order *begins* with the just ordering of love between man and woman. He divides his letter into two main parts. The first part explores the relationship between God's love (*agape*) and the love of the sexes (*eros*), while the second part offers a more concrete treatment of how the Church must exercise "love of neighbor" in creating a just society. While I limit the reflections of this book to the first part of the pope's letter, we must remember, as Benedict insists, that these two parts are "profoundly interconnected" (n. I). There's no place for division between Church teaching on sexual ethics and social justice. If we want to work for social justice, we must first do justice to the fundamental social unit: the relationship of man and woman and the family that springs from their love.

Eros *and* Agape

The ancient Greeks called the love between the sexes *eros,* from which we derive the term "erotic." Different historical and cultural contexts have supplied *eros* with various shades of meaning. In our day, that which is "erotic" has become almost synonymous with that which is "pornographic." As a result, many Christians seem to think the only proper response to *eros* is to avoid it, repress it, and stamp it out in favor of a "higher," more "spiritual" love.

This most certainly is *not* the approach Pope Benedict takes. Rather than surrendering *eros* to its many distortions, the pope reclaims *eros* by demonstrating its integral—and, tragically, forgotten—relationship with *agape.* In Christian usage, the Greek term *agape* came to describe the self-emptying, sacrificial love revealed in Christ. Two thousand years ago, Christianity produced a "revolution of love" in the social order, not because it rejected *eros* in favor of *agape,* but because it purified and infused *eros* with *agape.* From the earliest days of Christianity, St. Paul helped men and women understand that sexual union was a "great mystery" that referred to Christ's love for the Church (see Eph 5:31-32). Husbands were to love their wives *as Christ loved the Church*" (Eph 5:25). In other words, St. Paul taught that *eros* was meant to express *agape*.

But the great evangelist knew well that men and women are not able to integrate *eros* and *agape* on their own. This ability comes only as we are "strengthened with might through God's Spirit dwelling deep within us." It comes to those who, by grace, "know the love of Christ which surpasses knowledge" and are "filled with all the fullness of God." In turn, this "fullness of God" overflows in us to others. It becomes a "power at work within us" that "is able to do far more abundantly than all that we ask or think" (see Eph 3:16-20). St. Paul is speaking of the power of *agape*, the power to love as God loves. This power works in us not despite the physical and erotic realities of human life but *in and through them*.

This is the good news of the Gospel: Christ took on flesh *to redeem our flesh* by sharing with us *in his flesh* the love that truly satisfies. Reflecting on this truth, Pope Benedict helps us to see not only that Christians needn't reject *eros*, they *shouldn't* reject *eros*—indeed, they *mustn't*. Through ongoing purification, *eros* can and must become a path "towards authentic self-discovery and indeed the discovery of God" (n. 6). It is this discovery that brings each of us the love for which we so deeply long.

The Approach of This Book

A common complaint of those who wish to benefit from papal encyclicals is that these documents are not written for the average person. Pope Benedict's encyclical is not impenetrable, but its treasures need to be unpacked if the average person is to benefit more fully from them.

With that as my goal, I have pulled sixty-three key quotes from the first half of the encyclical (the part of the letter devoted to the relationship of *eros* and *agape*) and grouped them sequentially into nine topical chapters. I unfold each quote with a reflection. Over the course of the book, these reflections range in style from the more formal exposition of theological truths to the less formal and even informal sharing of personal stories and experiences. As you turn the following pages, you will also meet an interesting cast of characters. St. Augustine, Hugh Hefner, the Patriarch of Venice, Bono (lead singer of U2), my seven-year-old son, a self-professed "lesbian" I met on a plane, and Truman Burbank (of the movie *The Truman Show*) all make "guest appearances." But, more than anyone, John Paul II—a man who deeply understood the human heart and its craving for love—serves as a guide throughout.

Pope Benedict has stated that his "personal mission" is not to issue many new documents but to ensure that the teaching of his predecessor is embraced by the Church. *God Is Love*, although presented in a style that is clearly Benedict's, offers a beautiful continuation—even a crowning—of John Paul II's rich and extensive reflections on the love between the sexes. Those familiar with my work popularizing John Paul II's Theology of the Body may recognize some of the material I cover here. So that this book might stand alone, I have re-presented for those who are new to the subject matter several ideas that I developed elsewhere.

I offer these reflections on Pope Benedict's encyclical with the humble prayer that they will lead all who read them ever closer to the love that satisfies. May Mary, in whom the perfect integration of *eros* and *agape* already exists, guide all who read this book along the way of that integration.

–Christopher West

Chapter 1

ENCOUNTERING GOD
WHO IS LOVE

1. "'God is love, and he who abides in love abides in God, and God abides in him' (1 Jn 4:16). These words...express with remarkable clarity the heart of the Christian faith: the Christian image of God and the resulting image of mankind and its destiny" (n. 1).

What is your image of God? Is he an old man with a white beard ready to strike you down whenever you fail? Is he an anonymous force that set the universe in motion but cares little for his creatures? Is God a tyrant, a taskmaster, the ultimate law enforcer? And what, in your mind, is mankind's destiny? Is it cold earth six feet under? Or maybe a heavenly boredom of harps, clouds, and wings...*if* we're "good enough" to get there?

Listen to the *Catechism of the Catholic Church*'s description of God and of mankind's destiny: "God himself is an eternal exchange of love, Father, Son, and Holy Spirit, and"—here's the good part for us—"he has destined us to share in that exchange" (n. 221). *Love* outpoured in a rapture, happiness, and bliss that never end—this is the summary of God's mystery and the origin and destiny of the human being. If you've ever been madly in love, you've tasted a little bit of this mystery.

God *is not* a tyrant or an unrelenting taskmaster. As John Paul II insisted, the "paradigm of master-slave is foreign to the Gospel" (*CTH*, p. 226). God *is* love. Let that sink in. Let it wash away any notion of a tyrant, of a God who dangles a carrot in front of our noses but never lets us have it. God wants to satisfy our deepest desires for love. He planted those desires deep within us at the moment of our beginning. He gave us an unyielding thirst that, if we follow it, will lead us to the unyielding fountain. It will lead us to that living water that, if we drink it, we will never thirst again (see Jn 4:13-14).

But what does it mean to say God *is* love? While every explanation falls short of the divine mystery itself, we can recognize that God is love, not only because he loves us but also because *within God* the three Persons of the Trinity live an "eternal exchange of love." This "is the central mystery of Christian faith and life. It is the mystery of God in himself. It is therefore the source of all the other mysteries of faith, the light that enlightens them" (*CCC*, n. 234).

In the Church's language, God is an eternal *communion of Persons*. A "common union" (communion) of persons is established to the degree that persons mutually give themselves to one another in sacrificial love. Once again, no explanation of the Trinity suffices. Nonetheless, we can discern from revelation that the Father eternally "begets" the Son by *giving himself* to and for the Son. In turn, the Son (the "beloved of the Father") eternally receives the love of the Father and eternally gives himself back to the Father. This ever-shared, everspirating love *is* the Holy Spirit who, as we say in the Nicene Creed, "proceeds from the Father and the Son." Amazing. Stop to think about it. Perfect love—perfectly and eternally given, perfectly and eternally received, perfectly and eternally returned—that's God.

And here's why we exist: Love, by its nature, desires to expand its own communion. God certainly didn't *need* anyone else. The love of the Trinity is perfect and complete in itself. Yet out of sheer goodness and generosity, God wanted to create a great multitude of other persons to share in his own eternal "exchange of love."

This is why we're here. This is why we have all those deep longings and yearnings in our being—those cravings that just don't go away! St. Augustine said it best: "You have made us for yourself, O God, and our heart is restless till it rests in you."

2. "Saint John...offers a kind of summary of the Christian life: 'We have come to know and to believe in the love God has for us'" (n. 1).

What is the nature of the love God has for us? How are we to think of it? The Scriptures use many images to help us understand God's love for humanity: father and son, king and subjects, shepherd and sheep, vine and branches, head and body. Jesus even compares his love to that of a protective mother hen who wants to gather her chicks in the safety of her wings.

All of these images are helpful. But the Bible uses another image far more than these to describe God's love for humanity. It illuminates the mystery of God's love in a way that these images do not and cannot. Hence, it is the image favored by the greatest saints and mystics of the Church. In fact, it is not only an image or a metaphor. It is a sacrament. That means this image *truly communicates*—makes visible and real to us—the mystery of God's love that it symbolizes. We're speaking of the spousal image, the union of the bridegroom and the bride.

The Bible begins in Genesis with the marriage of the first man and woman, and it ends in Revelation with another "marriage": the marriage of Christ and the Church. The first human words recorded in the Bible are the words of a bridegroom's wonder and excitement as he beholds the unveiled beauty of his bride: "This at last is bone of my bones and flesh of my flesh" (Gen 2:23). The final human words recorded in the Bible are the words of the Bride's intense rejoicing at the coming of her Bridegroom: "The Spirit and the Bride say, 'Come'" (Rev 22:17).

The whole story of our salvation, the whole of biblical revelation, is contained "between" the love initiated by the Bridegroom and the response of the Bride. And so we have in these nuptial "bookends" a key for interpreting all that lies between. Through this lens we learn that God's eternal plan is to "marry" us—to live with us in communion: in an eternal exchange of love. If we take the analogy further, we see that, through this loving union, God wants to "impregnate" the Bride with eternal life, that is, he wants us lovingly to *conceive* his life within us and bear it forth.

Perhaps this sounds a bit shocking, even scandalous. But the idea of the heavenly Bridegroom giving life to the Bride lies at the heart of the Christian faith. And this idea of becoming "pregnant" with divine life is not merely a metaphor. Representing all of us, a woman once opened herself so profoundly to God's love that she literally—and, of course, virginally—conceived divine life in her womb. In this way, as the *Catechism* teaches, Mary perfectly fulfills "the spousal character of the human vocation in relation to God" (n. 505). In Mary, the Bride said *yes* to the eternal Bridegroom's proposal.

But there's more. God wanted this eternal "marital plan" to be so plain and obvious to us that he impressed an image of it in our very being by creating us male and female and calling us to become "one flesh." As St. Paul says, this union in one flesh is "a great mystery" that points to Christ's union with the Church (see Eph 5:31-32). Our bodies, then, are not only *biological*; they are also *theological*. Yes, our bodies are a "study of God" and his plan of love for the universe. As male and female, our bodies reveal the mystery of life-giving love and union that has been hidden in God from eternity. In other words, as Benedict points out in his encyclical, *eros* (human, erotic love) is meant to express *agape* (divine, sacrificial love).

Of course, none of this means that God is "sexual." We are made in God's image, not he in ours. God's mystery remains infinitely beyond the image of spousal love and union. At the same time, however, as John Paul II once observed, "There is no other human reality which corresponds more, humanly speaking, to that divine mystery" (*Homily*, December 20, 1988).

3. **"Being Christian is not the result of an ethical choice or a lofty idea, but the encounter with...a person, which gives life a new horizon and a decisive direction"** (n. 1).

The reduction of Christianity to a list of rules for living, to a moral code, is a terrible—indeed tragic—impoverishment of the Christian mystery. Obviously, following Christ places significant moral demands on us. But morality is not what Christianity *is*. Living a moral life is a fruit of having "encountered" the person of Christ.

The story of the woman caught in adultery is a good example of what Pope Benedict means (see Jn 8:2-11). Illicit sex can offer a quick fix of excitement, a sudden rush of emotion and physical release. But virtually everyone who has engaged in illicit sex can attest to that empty pit in the stomach that follows. This woman caught in the act of adultery went looking for love, intimacy, and affirmation from another, imagining perhaps that *this* time she would find what she was looking for. But, as always, the counterfeit couldn't satisfy.

It is in the midst of this feeling of emptiness and shame that she meets Christ. The angry crowd was anxious to stone her. Christ said whoever was without sin could cast the first stone. According to his own words, Jesus could have thrown a stone. But Jesus came not to condemn. He came to save (see Jn 3:17).

The gospel of John reports that "Jesus was left alone with the woman standing before him" (Jn 8:9). Here is the moment of "encounter with Christ" that, as Benedict says, "gives life a new horizon and a decisive direction." Reading into the story a bit, can we not imagine that, in this *face-to-face meeting* with Perfect Love, the woman found what she had been looking for in her previous sexual misadventures? Why was Christ so compassionate with sexual sinners, especially women? Could it be because he knew they were actually looking for *him*, the true Bridegroom, but they had been deceived by counterfeit loves? Sexual union—even when it is a beautiful expression of married love, and all the more so when it is not—can never satisfy the deepest ache of the human being for love and union. The best it can possibly be is a sacramental foreshadowing of the love that satisfies. That love comes only through Christ.

Having been saved from the counterfeit by the true Bridegroom, do you think when Jesus said, "Go, and sin no more" (see Jn 8:11), that this woman who had been caught in adultery turned and grumbled, "Who is this man to tell me what I can and cannot do with my body!?" Or do you think that, having tasted the love that satisfies, she received "a new horizon and a decisive direction"?

This "new horizon" is the penetrating realization that genuine love does, in fact, exist—that I needn't stifle my yearnings for a love that is lasting and real, nor settle for the counterfeits endlessly purveyed by our pornographic culture. This "decisive direction" is to follow Christ wherever he leads. Inevitably, Christ's "way" will take us to Calvary, through painful purifications and trials. But through them, we also enter the glory of resurrection, the glory of tasting truly what it means to be human, what it means to love. In turn, we experience the joy of sharing that love with others.

4. For the Christian, "love is now no longer a mere 'command'; it is the response to the gift of love with which God draws near to us" (n. 1).

If religion is man's search for God, Christianity, it has been said, is God's search for man. "In this is love, not that we loved God but that he loved us" (I Jn 4:10). God *always* takes the initiative in the Creator-creature relationship. This is why, in the analogy of the Bridegroom and the Bride, God is always the Bridegroom. The Bridegroom *gives* the seed, and the Bride opens to *receive* it. The Bridegroom *fathers* new life, and the Bride *mothers* it, conceiving it within herself, bearing it forth, and nurturing it.

This is not only biology; this is theology—theology *of the body*, to use John Paul II's famous expression. Our bodies in the intimacy of marital union are created to point us to the life-giving union of Christ and the Church (see Eph 5:31-32). When we encounter divine love, when we *experience* it and take it into ourselves, we are filled with new life, divine life. This divine life empowers us not only to "follow the rules" begrudgingly but also to fulfill God's law out of the overflow of love within us.

This means, among other things, that holiness is not first a matter of "doing" anything but of "letting it be done unto us." Holiness is the fruitfulness of *God's initiative* in us and *our response*. Holiness, as the *Catechism* teaches, "is measured according to the 'great mystery' in which the Bride responds with the gift of love to the gift of the Bridegroom" (n. 773). Why do we love to see marriage proposals in movies and those home-video television shows? Love offered and received warms the heart, for it is an image of the holiness we all long for.

5. "I wish in my first Encyclical to speak of the love which God lavishes upon us and which we in turn must share with others" (n. 1).

We cannot give what we don't have. We cannot share God's love with others if we haven't first allowed God to "lavish" his love upon us.

God is a gentleman. He does not impose his love on us. He awaits our freely given yes before he floods our hearts with his love. Alas, giving that yes is far more difficult than one might imagine. We have been trained from a very young age to hide our hearts, to shut down. We've been wounded, jaded by this selfish world. And so we're afraid to expose our hearts. We're afraid of being "naked," of being ourselves before others and even before God. We're afraid that God really isn't "love."

Be not afraid! Look to Christ, whose perfect love "casts out fear" (1 Jn 4:18). Christ's whole life is a testimony to the fact that God is love. In effect, his life says to us: "You don't believe God loves you? I will traverse the skies to show you how much God loves you. I will bleed myself dry to show you how much God loves you. I have not come to punish or condemn you, but to reward you with eternal life. It's okay. You are safe. Believe. You can remove your fig leaves in My presence. You can stand naked before Me without shame. I see you and I love you. Turn to Me and I will give you rest. Receive My love, abide in it, and let My love in you overflow to others, loving them as I have loved you."

> 6. "By contemplating the pierced side of Christ (see Jn 19:37), we can understand the starting-point of this Encyclical Letter: 'God is love' (1 Jn 4:8). It is there that this truth can be contemplated. It is from there that our definition of love must begin. In this contemplation the Christian discovers the path along which his life and love must move" (n. 12).

In the pierced side of Christ, we see the love of his heart *opened up* for us. Christ's heart pierced for his Bride, the Church: it is from here that our definition of love must begin. Let us turn, then, to the account of this piercing in the gospel of John. There we read that, to accelerate the death of the three men crucified that day, the Jews had asked Pilate to have their legs broken. This would cause their suffocation, since they would be unable to hoist themselves to breathe.

> So the soldiers came and broke the legs of the first, and of the other who had been crucified with him; but when they came to Jesus and saw that he was already dead, they did not break his legs. But one of the soldiers pierced his side with a spear, and at once there came out blood and water. He who saw it has borne witness—his testimony is true, and he knows that he tells the truth—that you also may believe (Jn 19:32-35).

Believe in what? Love. By contemplating the pierced side of Christ, we can understand that God is love. In this mysterious burst of blood and water, we witness *the explosion* of divine love in Christ's human heart. It is as if the membranes of his heart could no longer contain the fire of love within. The soldier's sword—intending to wound and ensure death—unleashed in time a new outpouring of the love that we find at the origin and foundation of the cosmos.

Many have asserted that Benedict's first encyclical is "uncontroversial." In an article entitled "Combing Through the Pope's First Encyclical," Peter Steinfels reflects on the pope's proclamation that love is the foundation of the cosmos and asks:

> Is this claim really uncontroversial? Humans, after all, have offered any number of ultimate characterizations of reality, from a swirl of atoms to a struggle for survival, from a war between matter and spirit to the search for pleasure and release, from the slow march of rationality to a cloud of illusion.
>
> There is plenty of evidence for each of these views. One can easily argue that the case for love, personal, self-giving love, as the bottom-line character of reality is the wildest, most astonishing of claims in the face of that evidence.
>
> At the deepest levels, is the parent caring for the ill or troubled child or the couple pledging mutual affection and support till death do them part going with the grain of the universe or acting in defiance of it? Is such love a flame that somehow begins and ends in a larger fire? Or is it a brief, bold flare that will ultimately be snuffed out in the darkness? (Associated Press, January 28, 2006)

Why is the idea that love is the foundation of the universe such an astonishing claim? What evidence refutes it? In a word: suffering.

It is impossible to comprehend the suffering of one human life, let alone the multiple billions of men, women, and children who have lived and died in the history of the earth. Wars, concentration camps, rapes, murders, starvation, betrayals, torture, child molestation, kidnappings, terrorism, natural disasters, unrequited love, disease, mental and physical disabilities, the unexpected (or even expected) death of loved ones, people ripped from family and homeland and sold into slavery—if "God is love," as Christian faith insists, how can he allow such suffering? Why is he blind to our misery?

Is he? By contemplating the blood and water (symbols of Eucharist and Baptism) gushing from the heart of this crucified God, we discover that God is rich in mercy. *Misericordia*, Latin for mercy, means "a heart which gives itself to those in misery" (*miseris cor dare*). God never promises to take away our sufferings in this life. But he promises to be *with us* in our misery. He promises us that we can *find him there* and that, in the end, he will bring great good out of our suffering.

He has already born our misery—all human misery from the beginning to the end of human history, including mine and yours—in his passion and death. And he rose again to show us that we, too, can live a new life, a life in which suffering has real value and redemptive meaning. In his final work, *Memory and Identity*, published just before his death, John Paul II wrote:

In sacrificing himself for us all, Christ gave a new meaning to suffering, opening up a new dimension, a new order: the order of love. It is true that suffering entered human history with original sin. Sin is that "sting" (see I Cor 15:55-56) which inflicts pain, wounding man mortally. Yet the passion of Christ on the cross gave a radically new meaning to suffering, transforming it from within. It introduced into human history, which is the history of sin, *a blameless suffering accepted purely for love.* This suffering opens the door to the hope of liberation, hope for the definitive elimination of that "sting" which is tearing humanity apart. It is this suffering which burns and consumes evil with the flame of love and draws forth even from sin a great flowering of good (*MI,* p. 167; emphasis added).

Can we even imagine "a blameless suffering accepted purely for love"? Christ was not "murdered." The nails did not hold him fast to the wood. He was the all-powerful Son of the Most High God. He could have come down from the cross at any moment. He could have prevented his torturers from ever touching him. He chose to suffer. He chose to stay on the cross. He chose to die. "No one takes [my life] from me, but I lay it down of my own accord" (Jn 10:18). This is "a blameless suffering accepted purely for love." Oh, the unfathomable depths of this love! Who can take it in?

Only from "within" this blameless suffering of the God-man— from within the flow of blood and water gushing from the heart of Christ—can we look at all the suffering in our hearts and in the world and still conclude that God is love. As John Paul II once wrote, "If the agony on the cross had not happened the truth that God is love would have been unfounded" (*CTH*, p. 66).

7. "To experience love and in this way to cause the light of God to enter into the world—this is the invitation I would like to extend with the present Encyclical" (n. 39).

Love is not merely an idea but an *experience*. It is *the* experience for which we are created and for which we long and search. This is why "man cannot live without love. He remains a being that is incomprehensible for himself, his life is senseless, if love is not revealed to him, if he does not encounter love, if he does not experience it and make it his own, if he does not participate intimately in it" (*RH*, n. 10).

Benedict invites us to discover the meaning of our lives by discovering and *experiencing* authentic love, not the counterfeit. Certainly we experience God's love in the love of others, in the beauty of creation, in the very fact of our existence. But we are invited to experience much more. We are invited to "encounter" the very Mystery behind the universe. We are invited to live in an intimate relationship with the God who created us, with the God who is love.

How is this possible? We are hopelessly earthbound. True, we cannot reach up to the heavens to encounter God. If God is all-powerful, though, he could, hypothetically, humble himself and come down to our level. But what are the chances of that?

"And the Word"—the *Logos*, the Logic and Wisdom at the core of the universe—"became flesh and dwelt among us" (Jn 1:14). This is the Christian claim: we do not need to shed our skin (as some world religions believe) to reach for the transcendent God. God took on our "skin"—he became flesh—to meet us where we are. "God comes to us in the things we know best and can verify most easily, the things of our everyday life, apart from which we cannot understand ourselves" (*FR*, n. 12).

The Church takes these "things we know best," the things we "can verify most easily"—things such as human conversation, human touch, the love of man and woman, water, bread, wine, oil — and, by the power of God, they become *sacraments*, visible, tangible continuations of and doorways into the mystery and miracle of God's Incarnation, of God's meeting us "in the flesh."

This Word made flesh is "the light of men. The light shines in the darkness, and the darkness has not overcome it" (Jn 1:4-5). Hence, as Benedict says, when we experience God's love, the light of God enters the world. Sacraments seem like empty religious rituals to many. Let us pray for the eyes to recognize the invisible, hidden treasures of the sacraments so that the light of God might enter our hearts and our world. How desperately our darkened world needs men and women ablaze with this divine light and love!

Chapter 2

DISTINGUISHING TRUE LOVE
FROM ITS COUNTERFEITS

8. In the "love between man and woman...human beings glimpse an apparently irresistible promise of happiness" (n. 2).

*H*ow is it, then, that the love between the sexes promises such happiness but leads so often to despair? Are we mistaken to look for happiness in erotic love? What light does the Gospel shed on any of this?

When some Pharisees questioned Jesus about the meaning of marriage, they recalled to him that Moses allowed divorce. Jesus' reply provides one of the keys to understanding the Gospel: "For your hardness of heart Moses allowed you to divorce your wives, but from the beginning it was not so" (Mt 19:8). In effect, Jesus is saying something like this: "You think all the tension, conflict, and heartache in the male-female relationship is normal? This isn't normal. This isn't the way God created it to be. Something has gone terribly wrong."

The *Catechism* tells us that "the disorder we notice so painfully [in the male-female relationship] does not stem from the *nature* of man and woman, nor from the nature of their relations, but from *sin*. As a break with God, the first sin had for its consequence the rupture of the original communion between man and woman" (*CCC*, n. 1607). That's the bad news. But here's the good news: "Jesus came to restore creation to the purity of its origins" (*CCC*, n. 2336). Therefore, by "following Christ, renouncing themselves, and taking up their crosses...spouses will be able to 'receive' the original meaning of marriage and live it with the help of Christ" (*CCC*, n. 1615). This is not idealism. This is a divine promise.

Men and women are not entirely mistaken in their attempts to seek happiness in the sexual relationship. But *eros* (human, erotic love) has no possibility of granting the happiness it promises if we kick *agape* (divine, sacrificial love) out of the picture. Where did Jesus perform his first miracle, and what was it? The newly married couple at Cana had run out of wine, and Christ restored it in superabundance. The "new wine" Christ offers at this marriage celebration is a symbol revealing the heart of his mission: Jesus came to restore the order of love in a world seriously distorted by sin. And the union of the sexes, as always, underlies the human "order of love."

Wine is a biblical symbol of God's love poured out for us. In the beginning, before sin, man and woman were "inebriated" with God's love. Divine love flowed from them and between them like rich, full-bodied wine. Since the dawn of sin, however, we have all "run out of wine." On our own, we don't have what it takes to love each other in a way that corresponds with our heart's true desire. And so, the man-woman relationship offers an "irresistible promise of happiness," but, lacking God's wine, it cannot deliver.

This is why the miracle at the wedding feast in Cana is such cause for rejoicing. Christ came to restore the wine to overflowing in man and woman's relationship—to infuse *eros* with *agape*. As we drink deeply from this new wine, we find ourselves empowered to love as we are called to love. In fact, winemaking is a fitting image for the process of allowing *eros* to be infused with and purified by *agape*. It can feel, at times, as if we are getting crushed and squeezed in the winepress. Then we must wait, patiently allowing the impurities to settle out. As we ferment, the juice of our lives is slowly transformed into wine. The longer we rest in the Lord's purifying love, the finer the wine.

9. "That love between man and woman which is neither planned nor willed, but somehow imposes itself upon human beings, was called *eros* by the ancient Greeks" (n. 3).

Can something imposed on us actually be love? Can something "neither planned nor willed" be worthy of the name "love"? Human experience attests that, for love to be love, it must flow from a person's freedom. In fact, God gave us freedom so that we might have the capacity to love (see *CCC*, n. 387).

Our culture talks a big line about "sexual freedom." But what does that mean in our culture? The culture says, "Do whatever you want with whomever you want whenever you want without ever saying no to your urge to merge." Does this promote freedom? Is an alcoholic who cannot say no to his next drink free? Or is he in chains? What our culture promotes as "sexual freedom"—

indulgence of instinct without restraint—is actually a sure path to sexual addiction.

I often ask my female students, "How many of you want to marry a man who cannot say no to sex?" (Notice, I don't ask the men if they want to marry women who cannot say no to sex. For whatever reason, women seem to recognize this truth more readily.) Never has a woman raised her hand. Women know intuitively that, if a man cannot say no to sex, his yes means nothing.

Why do we spay and neuter our dogs and cats? If we want to keep the pet populations down, why don't we just ask our pets to abstain? The answer is obvious: animals are not free to choose. They are ruled by instinct and, hence, cannot determine their own actions. As the *Catechism* observes, "Man's dignity...requires him to act out of conscious and free choice, as moved and drawn in a personal way from within, and not by blind impulses in himself or by mere external constraint" (*CCC*, n. 2339).

If erotic love is to lead to lasting happiness rather than to fleeting pleasure, it must flow from freedom and not merely from instinct. It is precisely for such freedom that Christ has set us free (see Gal 5:1).

10. "According to Friedrich Nietzsche, Christianity had poisoned *eros*....Here the German philosopher was expressing a widely-held perception: doesn't the Church, with all her commandments and prohibitions, turn to bitterness the most precious thing in life? Doesn't she blow the whistle just when the joy which is the Creator's gift

offers us a happiness which is itself a certain foretaste of the Divine? But is this the case? Did Christianity really destroy *eros*?" (n. 3, 4).

Nietzsche's opposition to Christian teaching on sexual morality—which, as Pope Benedict observes, a wide swath of humanity shares—could be summarized as follows: "Doing things the 'moral way' throws a wet blanket on the joy of sexual love. Right when one's mind, body, and soul are crying yes, the Church intervenes with her stifling, finger-wagging no. In this way Christianity poisons and destroys erotic love."

But let us seek to answer Benedict's question: Is this really the case? Does Christian morality *really* destroy the joy of erotic love? A puritanism that often passes for Christianity does. Puritanism is fear-based and repressive. Authentic Catholic morality *never* stems from puritanism. Could it be that the Church's prohibitions serve not to ruin our fun but to safeguard the hidden treasure of erotic love? Could it be that those who hold the Nietzschean view are actually duped by a counterfeit version of love and are missing out on this real hidden treasure?

The Nietzschean view of *eros* fails to recognize that we have fallen from God's original plan for sex. As a result of original sin, *eros* has been effectively cut off from *agape*. What's left is not the love that raises us to the heavens, but its cheap, debasing counterfeit: lust. Lust flares up in the human heart as an instinct in search of an outlet, as an "itch" that needs to be scratched. Many people, like Nietzsche, tend to think of this as the very nature of *eros*, but "from the beginning it was not so" (Mt 19:8). Before sin, man and woman experienced erotic desire not as a grasping for pleasure but as an aspiration toward all that is true, good, and beautiful. They experienced *eros* as the desire to love as God loves, to live in the mutual and sincere gift of self. Hence, they were both "naked and felt no shame" (Gen 2:25).

The biblical entrance of shame marks the beginning of lust (see Gen 3:7), of the separation of *eros* from *agape*. The Nietzschean view, having normalized this fallen experience ("Everybody does it"), fails to see that, far from "poisoning *eros*," the Church's teaching actually invites us to experience the full dimensions of *eros*—to allow *eros* to be purified by the divine fire of *agape*, the only love that truly satisfies our hunger.

Once we understand that *eros* without *agape* can never satisfy, then we can see that indulging lust is akin to eating out of a dumpster to satisfy our love-hunger. Why, though, would anyone ever eat scraps of garbage? It's better than starving, and most of us think that the dumpster is the only offering. We haven't heard or possibly haven't believed the good news of the Gospel. We haven't heard or believed that God offers us a lavish banquet of love. And so, thinking that garbage is our only hope for a meal, we grow embittered by the Church's prohibition: "Thou shalt not eat out of the dumpster." We fail to see that the Church's prohibition is simply the prerequisite for entering the mouth-watering banquet for which we are created.

Following the true path of Christ does not stifle *eros*; it purifies and redeems it. Yes, following Christ means refusing to indulge lust, but, as John Paul II wrote, this is only so we can "rediscover in what is 'erotic' the...true dignity of the gift. This is the role of the human spirit. ...If it does not assume this role, the very attraction of the senses and the passion of the body may stop at mere lust, devoid of ethical value." If men and women stop here, they do "not experience that fullness of 'eros,' which implies the upward impulse of the human spirit toward what is true, good, and beautiful, so that what is 'erotic' also becomes true, good, and beautiful" (*TOB* 48:1).

> 11. "The Greeks—not unlike other cultures—considered *eros* principally as a kind of intoxication, the overpowering of reason by 'divine madness' which tears man away from his finite existence and enables him, in the very process of being overwhelmed by divine power, to experience supreme happiness....In the religions, this attitude found expression in fertility cults, part of which was the 'sacred' prostitution which flourished in many temples. *Eros* was thus celebrated as divine power, as fellowship with the Divine" (n. 4).

The modern pornographic world seems to be repeating history. Wherever modern men and women worship—the mall, the TV, the computer, the movie theater, the sports stadium—the "temple prostitutes" are there to seduce us with offers of "supreme happiness." Sex has become the modern world's religion.

Yet, in recognizing the distortions of sex in our modern world, we mustn't throw out the baby with the bathwater. There is an important element of truth behind our society's idolatrous obsession with sex. *Behind every false god we discover our desire for the true God gone awry.* The sexual confusion so prevalent in our world and in our own hearts is simply the human desire for heaven gone berserk. If we untwist the distortions, we discover the astounding glory of human sexuality in the divine plan. "For this reason...the two become one flesh." For what reason? To reveal, proclaim, and anticipate the eternal union of Christ and the Church (see Eph 5:31-32).

The passionate union of man and woman in God's plan is meant to be an *icon*, an earthly sign that points us beyond itself to our eternal destiny of union with God. But when we lose sight of our destiny, when we lose sight of union with God as our ultimate fulfillment, we begin to pin all hopes for happiness on the earthly image. The icon then degenerates into an idol. We come to worship sex itself.

Sin involves confusing our desire for the *infinite* with finite things. Sexual union, as beautiful and joyous as it is meant to be in God's plan, always remains a finite thing. It can never satisfy our desire for the infinite. The best it can be is a foreshadowing, a foretaste, of that satisfaction. Hence, Jesus tells us that when the infinite is granted to us in the resurrection, men and women will no longer be given in marriage (see Mt 22:30). In other words, you no longer need an icon to point you *to* heaven when you're *in* heaven. This also explains why some people remain celibate "for the sake of the kingdom of heaven" (Mt 19:12). Most people are called to prepare for heaven in and through the sacrament of marriage. But Christ calls a small minority of men and women to "skip" the sacrament in order to devote all of their hungers and yearnings for love to the marriage that alone can satisfy: the "marriage" of Christ and the Church. When this marriage is lived in the spirit Christ intended, these men and women become a living sign that *heaven is real.* The eternal union of Christ and the Church is not just an idea or a theory; it is a living reality for which it is worth selling everything.

What should I do, then, when I recognize and live in my desire for the infinite? In seeking God, should I reject finite things? No! This is a classic blunder. The more we live in union with God even while here on earth, the more all the things of earth—including and, perhaps, especially the marital embrace—take on their true sacramental nature as foretastes of heaven. As we become more intimately united with Christ, all the pleasures of the earth, rather than being an "occasion of sin" as perhaps they once were, become so many icons pointing us to heaven. Even those who choose celibacy for the kingdom do not reject their sexuality (at least they are not supposed to!). They are meant to live it out in a different way, appreciating God's true plan for it as a foreshadowing of the marriage of Christ and the Church. That's why Benedict's reflections on *eros* and *agape* are meant for all men and women, regardless of their particular state or calling in life.

12. "The Old Testament...in no way rejected *eros* as such; rather, it declared war on a warped and destructive form of it, because this counterfeit divinization of *eros* actually strips it of its dignity and dehumanizes it" (n. 4).

Suppose I offered you the choice between a real million-dollar bill and a counterfeit. Which one would you want? The answer is obvious. But what if you were raised in a culture that incessantly bombarded you with propaganda convincing you that the counterfeit was the real thing and the real thing was a counterfeit? Might you be a little confused? Welcome to the world in which we live.

But people can live with counterfeit love for only so long. It *never* satisfies. Indeed, it wounds us *terribly*. The truth of the Church's teaching on sex, I suggest, can be confirmed in the wounds of a culture that has rejected it. This is why a culture that sells us counterfeit love must also—in order to keep the illusion going—offer us all kinds of numbing agents: alcohol, drugs, busyness, and the distraction of so much noise, to name a few. All of these numbing agents serve to keep us from listening to what our hearts are trying to tell us. Perhaps if we had the courage to remove the numbing agents from our lives and be alone before God with our pain, we would recognize that the "counterfeit divinization of *eros* actually strips it of its dignity and dehumanizes it." And we might also experience the consolation of a God who comes to us in our pain to heal and restore us.

13. "An intoxicated and undisciplined *eros*, then, is not an ascent in 'ecstasy' towards the Divine, but a fall, a degradation of man" (n. 4).

God gave us *eros*, I like to say, as the fuel of a rocket that is meant to launch us into the stars and beyond. Yet, what would happen if the engines of that rocket became inverted, no longer pointing us toward the stars but only back upon ourselves? Launch that rocket, and the result is a massive and self-destructive implosion.

Many Christians, having been burned by their own and others' "inverted rocket engines," think the solution is to reject the rocket, as if sexual desire itself were the problem. The rocket is *not* the problem. The problem is that the engines are pointed in the wrong direction. Authentic Christian teaching never attacks erotic desire itself. Rather, it seeks, by the grace of Christ's death and resurrection, to redirect our rocket engines toward the stars.

Although an undisciplined *eros* involves a fall and degradation, when erotic "passion is set into the whole of the spirit's deepest energies," John Paul II wrote, "it can also become a creative force; in this case, however, it must undergo a radical transformation" (*TOB* 39:2). Radical means "to the root." Through the graces of redemption, Christ restores the gift of sexuality *at its roots*, so that *eros* might, once again, become an incarnate expression of *agape*.

14. "Evidently, *eros* needs to be disciplined and purified if it is to provide not just fleeting pleasure, but a certain foretaste of the pinnacle of our existence, of that beatitude for which our whole being yearns" (n. 4).

Pope Benedict observes here that erotic love is *meant* to offer a kind of foretaste or foreshadowing of the supreme bliss that awaits us in heaven, "that beatitude for which our whole being yearns." We should pause for a moment to let that sink in.

No wonder we're all so interested in sex! The joy of the marital embrace—that simultaneously physical and spiritual, sensual and sacred moment when all is given in a sweet, ecstatic surrender of self to the other, when two solitudes commune and surrender their mingled life forces to the will of the Creator—this "great mystery" is meant to be a sign, a little glimmer of the ultimate purpose and reality of our existence: participation in the eternal mystery of love-generation found in the Trinity.

But, as Benedict observes, in order to experience the union of the sexes in this way, "*eros* needs to be disciplined and purified." Without such discipline and purification, all *eros* can offer is "fleeting pleasure." When mere pleasure is the goal, other people become the means. We end up *using* people rather than loving them. In fact, what we often call "love" in the relationship of the sexes, upon closer examination, amounts to little more than mutual using for pleasure; it amounts to little more than the indulgence of lust. And we can lust for more than just physical gratification. We can use another to boost our image, to gain financial stability, or for any number of reasons.

The person who is the object of lust soon realizes the sentiment of the other: "You don't need *me*. You don't love *me*. You're just looking for an opportunity to gratify *yourself*. You can get that from any number of people, or from your own fantasies and masturbation for that matter. What am I to you but an object for your pleasure? And what might become of me if you find someone who promises you more pleasure than I do?"

Far from feeling loved as an unrepeatable and irreplaceable person, whoever is the object of lust eventually realizes that he or she is being treated as a replaceable commodity. When *eros* is lived in this way, far from being a foretaste of the "beatitude for which our whole being yearns," it becomes instead a bitter taste of loneliness, alienation, pain, and even despair.

15. "Love promises infinity, eternity—a reality far greater and totally other than our everyday existence. Yet we have also seen that the way to attain this goal is not simply by submitting to instinct. Purification and growth in maturity are called for; and these also pass through the path of renunciation. Far from rejecting or 'poisoning' *eros*, they heal it and restore its true grandeur" (n. 5).

I once heard it said that to love someone is to tell that person that he or she will live forever. If God *is* love, then love, like God himself, is something eternal, infinite. Hence, if I give someone authentic love, in a sense I give that person eternity. If that person receives it, takes it in, and makes a permanent home for love in his or her heart, then that person will live forever.

Yet, as Pope Benedict rightly observes, authentic love is *very different* from submitting to instinct. If we tend to experience sexual desire as an instinct—a need that imposes itself on us, demanding an outlet—we must recognize that love demands mastery of that instinct. Only to the degree that a man and woman are masters of themselves are they capable of making a true gift of themselves. When sexual instinct imposes itself upon us, it can lead to acquiescence (that is, giving in to it) or it can lead us to act-from-our-essence. That "essence" is freedom. A person controlled by sexual instinct is not free. He or she is in chains.

"Self-mastery is a *long and exacting work*. One can never consider it acquired once and for all. It presupposes renewed effort at all stages of life" (*CCC*, n. 2342). It demands renunciation of lust, the warped and destructive form of *eros*. However, Christian renunciation does not involve the "annihilation" of anything authentically human. Christian renunciation involves a certain kind of "death," but *always* with a view to resurrection. Lust must die so that *eros* can be resurrected in its true grandeur. *Eros* loses nothing of its essence with the death of lust. Rather, it is liberated from what distorts it so that it might become what it truly is: a human way of expressing divine love.

Without setting our eyes on this restoration, or *resurrection,* of *eros,* we can conceive of renunciation only as Nietzsche did—as a "poisoning" of *eros,* as a great, big "no" that stifles the natural spontaneity of the sexual relationship. But this is a superficial perspective. The discipline required in living *eros* as a virtue (love) rather than as a vice (lust) does not stifle or harm the sexual relationship. Rather, it enlarges it, enriches it, liberates it, sublimates it, and beautifies it.

I once heard the following analogy given to explain the difference between the spontaneity of lust and love. Anyone can "spontaneously" bang on piano keys and make meaningless noise. A concert pianist can also spontaneously tickle the keys and make music that lifts the soul to the heavens. But everyone knows that behind the "spontaneity" of the concert pianist is a lifetime of quiet discipline, sacrifice, and renunciation. The spontaneity of an undisciplined *eros* can lead only to meaningless noise. The Christian view of *eros,* when properly understood and lived, instills the discipline that allows men and women to make spontaneous music that lifts them to the heavens.

The spontaneity of lust is thoughtless and self-focused, while the spontaneity of love is thoughtful and other-focused. Lust invades, while love invites. Lust, like banging on a piano, not only interrupts our peace of soul; it robs us of it. Love, like beautiful music, brings peace of soul to those who lack it and increases peace of soul in those who have it. But, again, such beautiful music comes only at the price of countless acts of sacrifice, countless unnoticed and private exercises of self-mastery. Only after countless hours of practicing the piano in solitude is the pianist prepared to share his gift with others.

Chapter 3

Unity of Body and Soul

16. "Man is truly himself when his body and soul are intimately united; the challenge of *eros* can be said to be truly overcome when this unification is achieved" (n. 5).

At one point during Luke Skywalker's training, Yoda, the all-knowing Jedi Master, pokes Luke on the shoulder with his cane and mutters in his classic half-Grover, half-Miss Piggy voice, "We are not this crude matter. Luminous beings are we." Well, Yoda, I hate to break it to you, but you're a heretic.

Contrary to widespread belief, the human being is not a spirit "trapped" in a body. The body is not a "prison" from which the soul will finally be liberated at death. Nor is the body "crude matter" housing our true "luminous" selves. In the authentic Christian view of things, the human being is an *incarnate spirit* or a *spiritualized body*.

As the *Catechism* teaches, "The unity of soul and body is so profound that one has to consider the soul to be the 'form' of the body: i.e., it is because of its spiritual soul that the body made of matter becomes a living, human body." Furthermore, "spirit and matter, in man, are not two natures united, but rather their union forms a single nature" (*CCC*, n. 365). It is only because of sin that we experience a rupture and disharmony between body and soul. "In the beginning," before our first parents fell into sin, the passions of the body harmonized perfectly with reason. The body submitted to the will's direction without conflict or rebellion. As a result of sin, however, "the control of the soul's spiritual faculties over the body is shattered." In turn, "the union of man and woman becomes subject to tensions, their relations henceforth marked by lust and domination" (*CCC*, n. 400).

When the passions of the body are detached from the aspirations and governance of the spirit, *eros* tends to have a will of its own, not unlike a rebellious child. It's not concerned with the dignity of the person and the truth of love. Its aim is gratification, pure and simple. So that *eros* can achieve its goal, the bodily passions will tyrannize the spiritual faculties, insisting on an outlet for pleasure, often relentlessly. The "challenge of *eros*," then, is precisely the challenge of integrating body and soul, so that the passions of the body and the aspirations of the spirit for truth, goodness, and beauty work together in an ever-deepening harmony.

This path of integration—moving daily to help *eros* surrender to the infusion of *agape*—is the task of an authentic Christian spirituality. But even here we often think in a disintegrated way. Authentic *Christian* spirituality is never lived at the expense of the body or in juxtaposition to it. *Christian* spirituality is always incarnational; it is always an *embodied* spirituality. To cut off our spiritual lives from our bodily lives is to render the Incarnation of God's Son meaningless in our lives. The Word made flesh *is* the healing of that tragic rift between matter and spirit. And it is precisely by appropriating the "redemption of the body" and "life in the Spirit" offered by Christ that we experience the reintegration of our own flesh and spirit (see Rom 8). The degree of this reintegration in us will be the measure of our ability to live and experience *eros* in its true splendor. This is Christ's gift to us, and He *longs* to grant us this gift of an integrated life.

> 17. "Should he aspire to be pure spirit and to reject the flesh as pertaining to his animal nature alone, then spirit and body would both lose their dignity. On the other hand, should he deny the spirit and consider matter, the body, as the only reality, he would likewise lose his greatness" (n. 5).

Lacking the reintegration of spirit and flesh to which we are called in Christ, we inevitably lean toward one side of the divide or the other, toward "angelism" or "animalism." One promotes a "spiritual" life at the expense of the body, and the other a "carnal" life to the neglect of the spirit.

Angelism views the human person as a spirit merely housed or even imprisoned in the body. Since the "real person" in this view is something purely spiritual, angelism not only considers the body external to the person; it tends to view the body as an obstacle to spiritual fulfillment. The angelistic moral code is rigorism; it condemns even some of the most natural manifestations of *eros* as impure. Hence, angelism tends toward prudishness and a fearful repression of sexual feelings and desires. Many Christians throughout history have fallen prey to this distortion. Even today people make the calamitous mistake of considering this "holiness." Christians who avoid laughter, music, color, beauty, humor, art, dancing, etc., as if it were a matter of "holiness" renounce joys that God longs for us to experience.

Animalism, on the other hand, stifles the spirit so that it can live a "carnal" life unhampered by the voice of conscience. Its moral code is permissiveness, which condemns any manifestation of temperance as a hindrance to freedom. Animalism promotes bodily pleasure as man's ultimate fulfillment. Hence, it encourages men and women to indulge their (disintegrated) erotic impulses without restraint, leading toward the indecent and the shameless. All we need to do is turn on the television or log on to the Internet to see how prevalent this distortion has become.

Cultural trends oscillate between these two extremes. Look at the twentieth century, for example. In 1900, a "respectable woman" wore about thirty-five pounds of clothing when she appeared in public. The sight of a woman's ankle could cause scandal. This is not healthy. Of course, at the end of the century men and women were appearing in public wearing next to nothing at all. This isn't healthy, either. What happened in the span of a hundred years? The wounds caused by the silence and repression of puritanism were enough to fuel a revolution. We call it, of course, the sexual revolution, but a more accurate description, I think, would be the "pornographic revolution."

When Hugh Hefner was asked why he started *Playboy* magazine, he said it was "a personal response to the hurt and hypocrisy of our Puritan heritage." Hefner elaborates:

Our family was...Puritan in a very real sense...Never hugged. Oh, no. There was absolutely no hugging or kissing in my family. There was a point in time when my mother, later in life, apologized to me for not being able to show affection. That was, of course, the way I'd been raised. I said to her, 'Mom...because of the things you weren't able to do, it set me on a course that changed my life and the world.' When I talk about the hurt and hypocrisy in some of our values—our sexual values—it comes from the fact that I didn't get hugged a lot as a kid (*Interview with Cathleen Falsani*, www.somareview.com).

When I first read this, I wanted to weep for this man. He, like the rest of the world, is simply starved for love and affection. His God-given yearnings to be touched, hugged, kissed, held, and affirmed were not met in healthy, holy ways, so he sought to satisfy them in other ways. It's a basic principle: If our hungers are not fed from the banquet, we will inevitably eat out of the dumpster.

You might find this surprising, but we as Catholics actually agree—or *should* agree—with Hugh Hefner's diagnosis of the disease of puritanism. The fear and rejection of the body and sexuality typical of puritanism is laced with interrelated heresies long condemned by the Catholic Church (dualism, gnosticism, spiritualism, Manichaeism, Jansenism, etc.). But if we agree with Hefner's diagnosis of this disease, Christians must disagree with his cure. Hefner's remedy doesn't, in fact, solve the problem of puritanism at all. All he did was flip the puritanical pancake over from repression to indulgence. *Both* approaches flow from the same failure to integrate body and soul, spirituality and sexuality.

Only through such an integration can we truly heal the wounds of puritanism. St. Paul called this cure the "redemption of the body" (see Rom 8:23). John Paul II called it living the theology of our bodies. And Benedict XVI calls it the unification of body and soul, *eros* and *agape*.

> 18. "It is neither the spirit alone nor the body alone that loves: it is man, the person, a unified creature composed of body and soul, who loves. Only when both dimensions are truly united, does man attain his full stature. Only thus is love—*eros*—able to mature and attain its authentic grandeur" (n. 5).

John Paul II expressed this same important truth in this way: "As an incarnate spirit, that is, a soul which expresses itself in a body and a body informed by an immortal spirit, man is called to love in his unified totality. Love includes the human body, and the body is made a sharer in spiritual love" (*FC*, n. 11). When we lack this integral understanding, love inevitably becomes either "angelistic" or "animalistic."

An angelistic "love" is a love afraid (often dreadfully so) of *eros* and its bodily expressions. Holding itself "above" the earthiness and messiness of flesh and blood, angelistic love masquerades as virtue, but it is really a front for vice. Lacking bodily expression, it traps love in a self-inflicted state of paralysis. Hence, angelistic love lacks color, warmth, and authentic joy. It remains cold, distant, aloof, prudish, and inhuman.

An animalistic "love," on the other hand, is a love afraid (often dreadfully so) of *eros*'s true demands. As such, it is also inhuman. Failing to submit itself to the spirit's longing for the eternal, animalistic love submerges itself in a never-ending deluge of temporal pleasures, demanding something from these that they can never supply—happiness, peace, contentment, satisfaction. (Why, we must ask, can't Mick Jagger get "no satisfaction"? Do we think for a moment that he's lacking sex?) Animalistic love thus locks its victims in a futile and escalating cycle of ever more varied and distorted indulgences, with the empty promise that this new pleasure will finally offer satisfaction, which it never does.

Love in its angelistic and animalistic mutations can never satisfy the longings of enfleshed spirits or "body-persons," such as we are. What the human being longs for, what the human being is created for, is *incarnate love*: a divine fire *in*-spiring the body and *ex*-pressed through it. This is why the Church joyously and boldly proclaims to the world that Christ—divine love-fire *incarnated*—is *the* answer to the human question (what a bold proposal!) and that the only way to find the love that satisfies is to "catch" this fire and allow it to burn away our impurities and to spread from us to others. In this way we learn to love as Christ loves.

How does Christ love? He gives us the fire of the Holy Spirit through *his body* "given up" for us. It is for *this* reason that "a man shall leave his father and mother and be joined to his wife, and the two shall become one flesh." For what reason? To image and participate *bodily* in the divine love-fire of Christ for his Bride, the Church (see

Eph 5:31-32). This, ultimately, is the "authentic grandeur" of *eros* about which Pope Benedict speaks.

19. "Christianity of the past is often criticized as having been opposed to the body; and it is quite true that tendencies of this sort have always existed" (n. 5).

Within the context of Benedict's admission that a tendency has existed within Christianity to oppose the body, it's important that we not confuse the mind *of* the Church with the mind of people *in* the Church. The mind *of* the Church has always defended the goodness of the body and of marital love against a great many heresies that have attacked it. Unfortunately, the Church's official condemnations of heresies such as Manichaeism, gnosticism, and Jansenism—all of which devalue the body and sexuality—seem to have had less of an impact on many minds than the heresies themselves.

The Church insists that "man may not despise his bodily life. Rather he is *obliged* to regard his body as good and to hold it in honor" (*CCC*, n. 364, emphasis added). Yet it is not difficult to find unflattering and even disparaging treatments of the body and sexuality in the writings of numerous historical Christian authors. Even today many people who have been raised in the Church and given a "good Catholic education" have come away considering their spirits "good" and their bodies "bad." Such dualistic, Manichaean thinking couldn't be further from the mind of the Church! Yet some would even claim the Bible itself teaches that the body is evil.

Professor Peter Kreeft observes how difficult it is for modern men and women to read the Bible correctly because of the dualism (the "split" between body and soul) that we have inherited from René Descartes' dictum "I think, therefore I am." As he keenly observes, "'Spiritual' to pre-modern cultures did not mean 'immaterial.' Pre-Cartesian cultures [cultures before the time of René Descartes] did not divide reality into two mutually exclusive categories of purely immaterial spirit and purely non-spiritual matter. Rather, they saw all matter as in-formed, in-breathed by spirit." Kreeft elaborates:

> Descartes initiates "angelism" when he says, "My whole essence is in thought alone." Matter and spirit now become "two clear and distinct ideas."...This is *our* common sense; we have inherited these categories, like non-removable contact lenses, from Descartes, and it is impossible for us to understand pre-Cartesian thinkers while we wear them. Thus we are constantly reading our modern categories anachronistically into the authors of the Bible (*EKH*, pp. 86-87).

For example, when St. Paul contrasts spirit and flesh, saying we should live by the former and not by the latter (see Rom 8 and Gal 5), he is not saying we should reject our bodies in favor of the spirit. In the incarnational view proper to him as a *Christian* apostle, he's saying we should welcome the Holy Spirit *in our bodies* so that what we do with our bodies will be *in-spired* by God. Like Christ, we are to *incarnate* God's life. We are to offer *our bodies* to God as a spiritual act of worship (see Rom 12).

To conclude that St. Paul is condemning the human body itself would be to accept a Manichaean mentality. Again, Manichaeism is a heresy that devalues the body. In fact, it considers the physical world to be the source of evil. In his Theology of the Body, John Paul II described the vast difference in the Manichaean and Christian views as follows: "While for the Manichaean mentality, the body and sexuality constitute...an 'anti-value,' for Christianity, on the contrary, they always remain a 'value not sufficiently appreciated'" (*TOB* 45:3). In other words, if Manichaeism says, "The body is bad," Christianity says, "The body is so good we have yet to fathom it."

Christianity doesn't "demonize" the body, as it is commonly claimed. Demons demonize the body, and then they blame the Bride of Christ for their own dirty work! Christianity *divinizes* the human body. Through the grace of the Incarnation, the human body is able to participate in the divine nature (see 2 Pt 1:4). In fact, the Catholic Church believes that *right now* a male and a female body (Jesus and Mary) participate in the eternal bliss of God's Trinitarian love. And the Church teaches that this is God's invitation to every *body*. Furthermore, the Church believes that the union of man and woman in "one flesh" is meant to be an earthly foretaste, a dim foreshadowing, of that eternal exchange of love. No one can possibly fathom the joy and union that await us. But the loving union of spouses provides a little window, a small glimpse. Let that sink in. Could there be a more exalted and glorious vision of the human body and the union of the sexes?

> 20. "The contemporary way of exalting the body is deceptive. *Eros*, reduced to pure 'sex,' has become a commodity, a mere 'thing' to be bought and sold, or rather, man himself becomes a commodity. This is hardly man's great 'yes' to the body. On the contrary, he now considers

his body and his sexuality as the purely material part of himself, to be used and exploited at will" (n. 5).

In our day we are witnessing a vast but false "cult of the body." We live in a pornographic world, a world that claims to exalt the body and sex. However, it does so in such a way that, in the end, men and women are not lifted up but degraded, often horribly so.

When we understand the authentic Christian vision of man and woman and their call to union, we realize that the problem with our pornographic culture is not that it overvalues the body and sex. The problem is that it has failed grievously to see how valuable the body and sex really are. *Eros* has been tragically *reduced* in the modern world, not exalted. It has been reduced, as Pope Benedict says, to "pure 'sex'"—that is, to something merely physical, to something cut off from the spiritual truth about man and woman and their eternal destiny of incarnate union with God himself.

Man becomes a commodity when sex becomes a commodity because sex—the body in its masculinity and femininity—expresses the heart and soul of man. The human body expresses the human *person*. What we do with and to our bodies, then, we do with and to our persons. We are not "ghosts in a machine," as the rock band The Police titled one of their albums. Matter matters. This is precisely what we fail to realize when we split the body and the soul apart. As John Paul II observed:

> The human family is facing the challenge of a *new Manichaeanism*, in which body and spirit are put in radical opposition; the body does not receive life from the

spirit, and the spirit does not give life to the body. Man thus *ceases to live as a person and a subject*. Regardless of all intentions and declarations to the contrary, he becomes merely an *object*. This neo-Manichaean culture has led, for example, to human sexuality being regarded more as an area *for manipulation and exploitation* than as the basis of that *primordial wonder* which led Adam on the morning of creation to exclaim before Eve: "This at last is bone of my bones and flesh of my flesh" (Gen 2:23). This same wonder is echoed in the words of the Song of Solomon: "You have ravished my heart, my sister, my bride, you have ravished my heart with a glance of your eyes" (Song 4:9). How far removed are some modern ideas from the profound understanding of masculinity and femininity found in divine revelation! (*LF*, n. 19)

If we do not reclaim this "profound understanding of masculinity and femininity found in divine revelation" civilization will eventually and inevitably collapse. This is why John Paul II's first major teaching project as pope was to proclaim the splendor of God's plan for the body and sexuality. And this is why Benedict's first encyclical echoes the same themes. Both popes seem to be saying not that the secular world overvalues sex but that *Christians don't value it enough*. If Christians understood and lived sexuality according to its true God-given value, they never would have allowed the pornographic revolution to occur. Or, one could argue that if Christians of the twentieth century had witnessed authentically to the true value of human sexuality, the pornographic revolution would have had no reason to occur.

21. Today, man does not see the body "as an arena for the exercise of his freedom, but as a mere object that he attempts, as he pleases, to make both enjoyable and harmless. Here we are actually dealing with a debasement of the human body: no longer is it integrated into our overall existential freedom; no longer is it a vital expression of our whole being, but it is more or less relegated to the purely biological sphere" (n. 5).

Doesn't the world trumpet sexual and reproductive "freedom"? How, then, are we to understand Pope Benedict's assertion that, today, man has separated his body from the "arena for the exercise of his freedom"? Obviously, we are dealing with two vastly different notions of freedom. John Paul II once wisely observed that "man understands his liberty according to whether he is free" (*BNA*, n. 97). In other words, one who is not truly free will understand freedom very differently from one who is.

The person who is *not* free will understand freedom as a "tossing off of the shackles" of the moral law so that he can indulge his fallen desires without restraint. His philosophy is "follow desire as it presents itself without hindering it." Does this make one free? Does this even make sense? Should I follow a desire to murder just because it presents itself? Would this make me free because I tossed off the oppressive law against murder and indulged my compulsion? Or, rather, would it demonstrate that I am actually enslaved by a compulsion to murder?

Such an idea of liberty is the freedom to "do what *feels* good," unhindered by the tyranny of law. The Christian understanding of liberty, on the other hand, is the freedom to "do what *is* good," unhindered by the tyranny of sin. In the Christian view, liberation is not the freedom *to* sin but the freedom *from* sin; it is freedom from the compulsion to commit sin. Freedom, then, is not found in indulging our compulsions but in *liberation from our compulsions to indulge*. Without this kind of freedom, love is impossible. All we can do is gratify our lustful instincts and call it "love." At its best, lust is a mere shadow of love. At its worst, it is love's antithesis, the using of another person as a means to my own selfish end, even if that end seems normal, natural, or deserved.

And, here again, the problem is one of lack of integration of body and soul. The integrated person understands liberty as freedom *from* sin; the disintegrated person insists that liberty is freedom *to* sin. (Of course, this sounds too negative, so we will inevitably redefine sin.) Sex, in this disintegrated view, becomes "more or less relegated to the purely biological sphere." We come to view sex through a plumber's lens as the coupling of random body parts. As such, sex becomes inhuman, animalistic, and, thus, a-moral—that is, outside the realm of moral responsibility, or, as Benedict puts it, divorced from the body as the "arena for the exercise of [true] freedom."

In the integral, Catholic view, "*sexuality* affects all aspects of the human person in the unity of his body and soul" (*CCC*, n. 2332). It "is by no means something purely biological, but concerns the innermost being of the human person as such" (*FC*, n. 11).

Which view corresponds more to the life we're looking for? Which view offers a better chance of finding the love that truly satisfies?

22. "The apparent exaltation of the body can quickly turn into a hatred of bodiliness" (n. 5).

When I typed "body hatred" into Google's search engine, a list of over fourteen million websites, articles, and other references appeared. Does anyone doubt that our culture's brand of "exalting the body" has led countless men and women to be dissatisfied with their own? Why is the cosmetic-surgery industry exploding? Why do so many people have eating disorders? Why do so many of us feel uncomfortable in our own skin and displeased with the way we look? One of the main reasons is that the bodies the culture exalts are airbrushed fantasies and computer-altered ideals: bodies without blemishes; bodies without an ounce of fat; bodies that, in all truth, no one has, not even the models who pose for these doctored photographs.

We are constantly told by the media: we are too fat or too thin; we are too short or too tall; we are too flabby or too wrinkled; we have too much body hair or not enough; our eyes, skin, or hair are the wrong color; our faces are too blotchy; our complexions are not smooth enough; various body parts should be bigger or smaller, rounder or flatter, firmer or softer. In short, we are constantly told to scrutinize virtually every aspect of our anatomy. Because of the airbrushed ideals exalted by our culture, we inevitably find our own bodies wanting.

But fear not! For every bodily "flaw" the media brainwashes us into believing we have, that same media will sell us some product or procedure to correct it. From breast implants to hair transplants, from exotic skin creams to stranger-than-fiction exercise machines, from buttocks reduction by liposuction to abs of steel for sex appeal: these are the new "sacraments" and "liturgical rituals" of a false cult of the body. And, as is the case with every cult, the followers remain at the mercy of their leaders, the reigning high priests and priestesses of the cult(ure) who dictate to them how they should look and live. Hatred toward our own bodies is a sure sign that we have believed the cult leaders' lies.

The lyrics of the song "Good Sons and Daughters" by a secular rock band called the Rainmakers sum up well the tragedy of believing the message of this false "cult of the body":

> We were true believers that this song of gold
> Was a high holy fever that purified the soul
> But peace turned to chaos, equality a laugh
> As girls danced a-go-go to our golden calf
>
> The revolution came, the revolution went
> Not meant for all, just that fifty percent
> That drew the dots from pin-ups and porno to rape
> And bought into Hollywood and Hefner's sly hate

If this "sly hate" has blinded you to the true goodness and beauty of your body, the good news is that Christ came preaching sight for the blind. Perhaps the following prayer might help open a path to healing.

Jesus, Word made flesh, give me the grace to confront the lies I have believed, the lies that have lodged in my heart that make it so difficult for me to love, accept, and understand my body as God created it to be. Dislodge these lies from my heart and replace them with the glorious truth that my body shares in the divine image, that my body is a sign of your own goodness, your own love, your own life, your own beauty. Let it be, Lord, according to your Word. Amen.

Chapter 4

TRUE *EROS*

23. It is true that *"eros* tends to rise 'in ecstasy' towards the Divine, to lead us beyond ourselves; yet for this very reason it calls for a path of ascent, renunciation, purification and healing. Concretely, what does this path of ascent and purification entail? How might love be experienced so that it can fully realize its human and divine promise? Here we can find a first, important indication in the *Song of Songs,* an Old Testament book well known to the mystics" (n. 5-6).

T he Song of Songs, the Old Testament's ode to erotic love, is often cast as an allegory of God's spiritual love for His people. It is that, but it is also an unabashed biblical celebration of the bodily, erotic love of spouses. In this celebration of *eros*—not despite it—we catch a glimpse of something divine. The sexual love celebrated in the Song of Songs, however, is not an abandonment to lustful instinct. It is an *eros* that flows from a profound integration of body and soul in each of the lovers. It is an *eros* filled to overflowing with *agape.* In other words, it is an *eros* reaping the rich, lasting fruits of inner purification.

Let us seek to offer a preliminary answer to Pope Benedict's question: "Concretely, what does this path of ascent and purification entail?" First and foremost, it demands a firm commitment of the will to uphold the supreme value and goodness of the body and sexual relations against all that threaten them. This, of course, presupposes a clear recognition and interiorization of the body's actual value and goodness. A person who doesn't appreciate the value of a vintage bottle of wine will not care if it goes to waste or spoils. But the wine connoisseur is anxious to safeguard his prized Bordeaux.

Because of the deep-rooted tendencies of angelism and animalism in our culture and in most of our upbringings, we are in need of ongoing healing if we are to understand, see, and "feel" the great dignity God has bestowed on us in creating us male and female and calling us to union. Hence, if we are to journey on the "path of ascent and purification," we must, above all, pray fervently for God's light to flood our minds and hearts with truth. We need not conform to this world: we can be transformed through the renewal of our minds (see Rom 12:2).

To the degree that we have interiorized the supreme value and goodness of the body and sex, we find the heart's true motivation for renouncing lust. Renunciation in the sexual sphere, if it is to lead to virtue, must be motivated not by fear or disdain for sex, nor merely by the imposition of a law or moral code. It must be motivated by *love*: love for God, love for oneself, love for others, and love for the goodness and beauty of sex itself. Otherwise, renunciation will not lead to freedom and virtue, but to interior frustration, inevitable relapse, and, eventually, further rebellion.

As Karol Wojtyla, the future John Paul II, wrote in his book *Love and Responsibility*, "*Chastity can only be thought of in association with the virtue of love*. Its function is to free love from the utilitarian attitude." It must control "those centers deep within the human being in which the utilitarian attitude is hatched and grows" (*LR*, pp. 169, 170). If it does not control those lustful tendencies, then sexual relations will not be an expression of love. On the contrary, they will be a negation of love—merely a response to a utilitarian instinct for pleasure at another's expense.

But here "control" must not be thought of merely as the caging of a wild beast. If, at first, lust must be "contained" by force of will, as one progresses on the path of virtue, the beast is gradually transformed so that it no longer needs a cage. Mature chastity is not a white-knuckled effort to suppress one's lustful impulses. Mature chastity *liberates us from lustful impulses*, enabling us to see others rightly and become a free and sincere gift to them. To the degree that men and women experience liberation from the utilitarian attitude of lust, they come to appreciate the beauty and mystery of sexuality with a depth, nobility, and intensity altogether unknown to lust. Lust, in fact, becomes distasteful to men and women who discover this freedom (freedom to love) in the same way that cheap wine becomes unpalatable to the person who grows in appreciation of the good stuff.

It is precisely for such freedom that Christ has set us free (see Gal 5:1). How do we experience this freedom? It is granted to the degree that we open ourselves to the grace of Christ's death and resurrection, allowing it to permeate us in order to transform us. Lust must be "crucified" in us so that we can walk in a redeemed,

or "resurrected," experience of sexual desire. As I wrote in my book
Theology of the Body for Beginners,

> Growing in purity certainly demands human effort, but
> we're also aided by supernatural grace. Here it's crucial
> to distinguish between indulgence, repression, and
> redemption. When lust "flares up," most people think
> they have only two choices: indulge or repress....Yet there
> is another way! Rather than repress lust by pushing it
> into the subconscious, trying to ignore it, or otherwise
> seeking to annihilate it, we must *surrender* our lusts to
> Christ and allow him to slay them. As we do, "the Spirit
> of the Lord gives new form to our desires" (*CCC*, n.
> 2764). In other words, as we allow lust to be "crucified,"
> we also come to experience the "resurrection" of God's
> original plan for sexual desire. Not immediately, but
> gradually, progressively, as we take up our cross every
> day and follow, we come to experience sexual desire as
> the power to love in God's image (*TBB*, pp. 49-50).

The answer, then, to Benedict's question, "Concretely, what
does this path of ascent and purification entail?" is that it entails
the cross. It entails our willingness to carry in our own bodies "the
death of Jesus, so that the life of Jesus may also be manifested in our
bodies" (2 Cor 4:10).

This is a hard sell. The luring temptations of angelism and
animalism can seem like attractive alternatives to the pain of being
"crucified with Christ." But where else can we go? Jesus has the
words of eternal life. And he beckons us: "Follow me!"

24. *Agape* "expresses the experience of a love which involves a real discovery of the other, moving beyond the selfish character that prevailed earlier. Love now becomes concern and care for the other. No longer is it self-seeking, a sinking in the intoxication of happiness; instead it seeks the good of the beloved: it becomes renunciation and it is ready, and even willing, for sacrifice" (n. 6).

Authentic love (*agape*) does not say, "I long for you as a good," but "I long for your good; I long for that which is good for *you*." The person who truly loves longs for this with no ulterior motive or selfish consideration. This is the purest form of love and, without doubt, it brings the greatest fulfillment (see *LR*, pp. 83-84). It is the love every human being desires. It is the love that leads to a real discovery of and delight in *the person*.

A self-seeking love never leads to that "real discovery of the other," of which Benedict speaks, since such a love is not truly interested in *who the other is*, but only in how the other is useful or pleasing *to me*. Love can only reach maturity when it surpasses how the other person makes me *feel* to arrive at who the other person *is*. This means that authentic love is attracted not just by attributes or qualities of a person that light a "spark" in me. Such attraction, if it is properly directed, may lead to love, but it is not yet love. Conversely, such attraction, if it is not properly directed, will lead not to love but to its direct opposite: lust, the using of another person to satisfy my own selfish needs. Love, as Pope Benedict observes, must move "beyond the selfish character that prevailed earlier" to become "concern and care for the other" as an unrepeatable person.

Qualities and attributes are *repeatable*. Any number of people with the "right" qualities can ignite that enchanting spark in me. The person, however, is *unrepeatable*. No person can ever be compared to, measured by, or replaced by another. This is why infidelity—even committed "in the heart" (indulging in pornography would be a prime example)—is so bitterly painful. It says to the other: "You are repeatable; you are replaceable."

Paraphrasing the Italian ethicist Rocco Buttiglione, we can recognize that lovers often experience sexual stimuli offering equally or more seductive possibilities of new sexual relationships. If any real caring I have for a person gives way in the end to his or her being only an instrument for my own pleasure, then he or she can easily be replaced in such a function, a fact that casts a permanent shadow of doubt over the relationship. The case is different, Buttiglione observes, when love reaches the person. Then the other is loved not for the quality that he or she has (and which one can lose or which others could have in a higher degree) but simply for his or her own sake. Only then is their life together something more than the joining of two selfish individuals. Only then are they capable of achieving a real personal unity (see *KW*, p. 102).

And only then has love reached a sure foundation. As Buttiglione asserts, "Only the value of the person can sustain a stable relationship. The other values of sexuality are wasted away by time and are exposed to the danger of disillusion. But this is not the case for the value of the person...which is stable and in some way infinite. When love develops and reaches the person, then it is forever" (*KW*, p. 100). And *that's* the love we all want!

25. "It is part of love's growth towards higher levels and inward purification that it now seeks to become definitive, and it does so in a twofold sense: both in the sense of exclusivity (this particular person alone) and in the sense of being 'for ever.' Love embraces the whole of existence in each of its dimensions, including the dimension of time. It could hardly be otherwise, since its promise looks towards its definitive goal: love looks to the eternal" (n. 6).

Despite the media's incessant mockery of permanent, committed love—marriage—the human heart still cries out for a love that lasts forever. How many romantic poems and love songs attest to this? The Church's teaching that the love of man and woman is fulfilled only in a lifelong commitment is not an imposition upon the human heart but a confident affirmation of what the human heart yearns for, even if the fulfillment of that yearning presents innumerable challenges.

The heart's longing for a lasting love between man and woman points to the human yearning for the God, who is eternal love. Here we also catch a glimpse of the sacramentality of marriage. Sacraments are earthly foreshadowings of heavenly mysteries. They are signs in the here and now that truly communicate divine realities to us, but only to the degree that they accurately signify divine realities. When man and woman become "one flesh" in the sacrament of marriage, their union is a "great mystery" that truly reveals and communicates the union of Christ and the Church (see Eph 5:31-32). When spouses divorce, the equivalent in sacramental terms is that Christ has abandoned the Church (or the Church has abandoned Christ). This is not only unthinkable; it is not only impossible; it is blasphemous.

To divorce the Church from Christ or Christ from the Church introduces a rupture into the very foundations of the cosmos.

The Church, following the words of Christ himself, has always taught that "whoever divorces his wife and marries another, commits adultery against her; and if she divorces her husband and marries another, she commits adultery" (Mk 10:11-12). The disciples, recognizing the difficulties involved in remaining with one person for life, grumbled that, if this were the case, it would be better not to marry at all (see Mt 19:10).

This, in fact, is an accurate assessment of the situation if men and women were left to their own resources to carry out the Lord's design. Men and women find themselves in a tragic bind when they embark on marriage. They yearn for a love that lasts forever, but on their own they don't have the resources to see it through. We have all, as stated previously, run out of the "wine" that empowers us to love as God loves (forever). But if spouses, like the couple at Cana, invite Jesus and Mary to be part of their love (see Jn 2:1-2), they will find themselves with an overflow of wine, empowering them to live what they so ardently desire, a love that stands the test of time and prepares them for their definitive goal: eternal love. This is the true grandeur of *eros*. As it is purified and infused with *agape*, it points us towards eternity, infinity, the fulfillment of every human aspiration and desire.

26. "Love is indeed 'ecstasy,' not in the sense of a moment of intoxication, but rather as a journey, an ongoing exodus out of the closed inward-looking self towards its liberation

through self-giving, and thus towards authentic self-discovery and indeed the discovery of God" (n. 6).

In a key passage from the Second Vatican Council, we read that "man, who is the only creature on earth which God has willed for itself, cannot fully find himself except through a sincere gift of himself" (*GS,* n. 24). This is another way of saying that love is man's origin, vocation, and destiny. The human being was created *from* love and *for* love. Apart from love, the human being cannot find himself. He does not know who he is. He has no true identity apart from love.

God did not create us for *his* sake. Why would he need us? He is perfect in his own Trinitarian exchange of self-giving love. God created us for *our own* sakes, in total generosity, so that he might bestow on us a share in his own bliss. Our existence is a sheer gift, given so that we might experience God's self-giving love. Gift. *All is gift.* If we let this truth sink in, it changes *everything.* It becomes the starting point of "an ongoing exodus out of the closed inward-looking self towards its liberation through self-giving," as Pope Benedict says.

How many of us have images of heaven in which the saints, in slave-like fashion, will be fanning God with massive palm branches while he reclines on his throne? God doesn't need slaves to take care of his needs. God has no needs! If it is true that we are created to "serve God," the service we render God, believe it or not, is first *to allow him to serve us.* Do we forget that Christ came not to be served but to serve (see Mt 20:28)? As St. John of the Cross taught, what we give back to God is precisely what he has first given us—his love, his Holy Spirit. In this way, we, too, are caught up in the eternal exchange of love between the Father and the Son, which *is* the Holy Spirit.

Furthermore, if it is true that we exist for God's glory, this is not so that we can glorify God (what, as creatures, can we possibly add to God's glory?) but so that *he can glorify us*. As the *Catechism* explains, quoting St. Bonaventure, "God created all things 'not to increase his glory, but to show it forth and communicate it,' for God has no other reason for creating than his love and goodness" (*CCC*, n. 293). Happiness, therefore, comes not by grasping at it but by *receiving* the gift God has desired to give us from all eternity. And the more we receive life as gift, the more we want to live as the same gift to others that life is to us. Only in this exchange of *receiving* and *giving* the divine gift (love) do we discover who God is and who we are.

God is self-giving love, and we are created from this love so that we can receive it and share it with others. The real epiphany comes when we realize that an image of this "great mystery" is stamped in our very bodies! Sexual difference is the most concrete expression of "gift" in the created world. A man's body makes no sense by itself, nor does a woman's. Only when one body is seen in light of the other do we discover the unmistakable plan of the Creator and the call to be "gift." You've heard some women complain, "He thinks he's God's gift to women." Well, in this sense, he—and every man—is precisely that. And women are God's gift to men. God has given men and women to each other to mirror the eternally faithful, generous, generating exchange of love found in the Trinity. John Paul II called this the spousal meaning of the body. It is the body's *"power to express love: precisely that love in which the human person becomes a gift* and—through this gift—fulfills the very meaning of his being and existence" (*TOB* 15:1).

If we are ever to live *eros* as a path of true ecstasy, we must learn to "read" the true language of our bodies. Our bodies proclaim a great mystery. They are not only biological. They are also, and even more so, *theological*. They speak about who God is, who we are, and who we are called to be. As John Paul II wrote, "This is *the body: a witness to creation as a fundamental gift, and therefore a witness to Love as the source from which this same giving springs.* Masculinity-femininity – namely, sex—is the original sign of [God's] creative donation...This is the meaning with which sex enters into the theology of the body" (*TOB* 14:4).

> 27. "'Whoever seeks to gain his life will lose it, but whoever loses his life will preserve it' (Lk 17:33)....In these words, Jesus portrays...the essence of love and indeed of human life itself" (n. 6).

While watching the ski-jumping event during the 2006 Winter Olympics, I heard the television commentator observe that "the key to ski-jumping is getting your body to do something that your brain tells you is suicide." Right when every hardwired, self-preservation instinct is screaming at you to pull back ("Abort! Abort!"), you have to thrust yourself headlong into icy thin air.

It's an apt metaphor. Life is like a ski jump. We must "lose ourselves," we must fight every self-preservation instinct (most of these, it seems, are really *"selfish* preservation instincts") and, with an act of faith, we must thrust ourselves headlong out over the precipice. As the commentator added, "You must be aggressive from the takeoff, and that's where it can really be scary." Uh-huh.

But what are we really clinging to, anyway? What is it we're so afraid to let go of, so afraid to "lose"? Whatever it is, it's holding us back from the sumptuous banquet served to us by the One who gave us the hunger and who alone knows the recipe to satisfy it. For failure to believe in so great a gift, we cling to putrid scraps from a dumpster. We cling to soiled rags when Christ offers us royal robes. We cling to finite things when Christ offers us infinity. We cling to NOW when Christ offers us eternity.

And here's the weight of being human: God respects our choices. If we say, "Thanks, but no thanks, I prefer the dumpster; I prefer the rags; I prefer finite pleasures," he will not force-feed us. The burden of being human is the freedom to choose between good and evil. Ultimately this means we must choose between heaven and hell. Why do we cling to the garbage, the rags, the fleeting pleasures? Why would anyone ever choose hell? Because we don't believe in the gift. At some deep level, we don't believe that God is love. We might think we believe, but in the end we often don't trust that God wants to *give us* the eternal wine of satisfaction. So we grasp at the cheap stuff and, with it, we numb ourselves to the pain that inevitably results.

The answer we give to the following question—although we tend to do so at a deep, non-cognitive level—determines the essential paradigm of our lives: Do we believe that God is love, that he is gift, that he wants to grant us the deepest desires of our hearts for happiness? If so, then we are ready to "lose ourselves" in order to "find ourselves." This is "the paradigm of gift." To experience the happiness for which we yearn, we need only open to the gift in faith. For "*faith*, in its deepest essence," John Paul II told us, "is *the openness of the human heart to the gift: to God's self-communication in the Holy Spirit*" (*DV*, n. 51, emphasis added).

At the other end of the spectrum is "the paradigm of denial." God denies the satisfaction of our yearnings for happiness because, in this paradigm, God is *not* love, God is *not* gift. He does *not* want to share his life with us. To experience the happiness for which we yearn, we must ignore God, bargain with or manipulate him, or even battle against him. In turn, we end up clinging to whatever scraps of pleasure we can find in this finite world because, at a deep, unconscious level, we believe that this is all there really is. Moreover, since the supply is finite, we will tend to look on others as competitors. No infinite gift for sharing exists, only a finite supply of the earth's resources and pleasures, which six billion people are grasping at, fighting over, and hoarding whatever they can get their hands on.

The Christian paradigm is radically different. It says open your hands, let go of all you've grasped and hoarded and clung to, and you will be given as a free gift all that you truly desire. Sell all you have, give the money to the poor, and you will have infinite treasures. Lose your life, and you will find it. Give yourself away freely and totally, and you will *re*cover and *dis*cover your true self. Do precisely what your brain says is suicidal, and you will soar, vivified with new life beyond your wildest imaginings. Open yourself to the gift of infinity, and it will be freely given to you.

Here's the human conundrum in a nutshell: We are created with a desire for infinity, but, as finite creatures, we have no access to it on our own. This places us in a position of *radical dependence* on the Infinite One to grant us the gift of himself, his own infinity. Do we believe he will? Do we trust in the gift? That is the question. Everything turns on our answer.

The world does not believe in the divine gift. Herein lies the world's sin and all personal sin. This "denial of the gift" is the beginning of all suffering, of all evil, of every human tragedy. Christ enters this world of denial with the specific mission of refuting its basic paradigm by affirming with his bodily life, death, and resurrection that *God is gift*. I suggest that, when the Christian proposal is presented in all its splendor, people resist it not because it's too hard but because it's too good to believe. That's the real stumbling block when the Gospel is preached in its fullness. Perhaps this is why Jesus' first words in his public ministry were "Repent, and believe in the gospel" (Mk 1:15).

And it bears repeating: God inscribed a sign of this good news right in our bodies by creating us male and female. Whether we seek to gain our lives or lose our lives, therefore, will be determined to a large extent by the way in which we "live our bodies," the way in which we live *eros*: as something either self-giving or self-serving.

Chapter 5

THE MEETING OF
EROS AND *AGAPE*

28. If the distinction between *eros* and *agape* were "to be taken to extremes, the essence of Christianity would be detached from the vital relations fundamental to human existence, and would become...decisively cut off from the complex fabric of human life" (n. 7).

*P*ope Benedict speaks here of the interconnection between "the essence of Christianity" and those "vital relations fundamental to human existence": sexual relations. Furthermore, he says that this interconnection depends upon the proper interconnection of *eros* and *agape*. Let's explore this idea.

At the essence of Christianity we discover the mystery of a Trinitarian God, three divine Persons who live a perfect "unity-in-distinction." This means that each divine Person is fully unified with the others in the one divine Life, yet each divine Person is distinct from the others. The Father is not the Son or the Holy Spirit, the Son is not the Father or the Holy Spirit, and the Holy Spirit is not the Father or the Son. Each distinct Person is fully God, not partially God, but there are not three Gods. The *three* distinct Persons are *one* God. This is some dense theology. It is also "the central mystery of Christian faith and life. It is the mystery of God in himself. It is therefore the source of all the other mysteries of faith, the light that enlightens them" (*CCC*, n. 234).

For example, we see how God's own "unity-in-distinction" as Trinity illuminates the mystery of the Incarnation. "The unique and altogether singular event of the Incarnation of the Son of God does not mean that Jesus Christ is part God and part man, nor does it imply that he is the result of a confused mixture of the divine and the human." Christian faith believes that the second Person of the Trinity "became truly man while remaining truly God. Jesus Christ is true God and true man" (*CCC*, n. 464). His divine and human natures are perfectly united without blurring their distinction (see *CCC*, n. 465-469).

What Pope Benedict teaches about the proper relationship between *eros* (human love) and *agape* (divine love) is deeply rooted in the mystery of the Incarnation and, in turn, the Trinity. *Eros* is distinct from *agape*, just as the human nature in Christ is distinct from the divine. Furthermore, just as the human and the divine natures in Christ are profoundly and indissolubly united, so are erotic and divine love (or, at least, they should be). Indeed, the proper unity of *eros* and *agape* flows precisely from the mystery of the Incarnation, in which the human and divine meet in an embrace that never ends.

An attack on the unity of *eros* and *agape*, be it of the animalistic (keep holiness out of my sex) or angelistic (keep sex out of my holiness) variety, is ultimately an attack on the Incarnation, on the interpenetration of humanity and divinity in the womb of Mary.

Here we are unmasking the precise goal of the enemy. The antichrist seeks any and every means to deny that Christ has come in the flesh (see I Jn 4:2-3). Denying the unity of *eros* and *agape* is one hell of a way to do it.

Sexual relations, those "vital relations fundamental to human existence," as Benedict put it, become detached from Christianity precisely in the measure that we detach erotic love from divine love. In this same measure, Christianity becomes "decisively cut off from the complex fabric of human life" and isn't really Christianity at all. It becomes something we might dabble in on Sunday morning but has little or nothing to say to us during the rest of the week, least of all in our sexual lives. "Keep God out of the bedroom" is the widespread sentiment coming from those in the world. And, tragically, "Keep sex out of the Church" has been a common complaint of many people in the pews.

If God is love, then what is sex if we block God out of it? It can't be love. And if sex is a "great mystery" that refers to Christ and the Church (see Eph 5:31-32), then what is the Church if we block sex out of it? It can't be the Church of the Incarnate Christ. The challenge, then, of integrating *eros* and *agape* is the challenge not only of understanding what sex truly is in the divine plan, but also of understanding who God truly is when he united himself with our flesh.

29. *Eros* and *agape* "can never be completely separated. The more the two, in their different aspects, find a proper unity in the one reality of love, the more the true nature of love in

general is realized." As *eros* matures, it "is concerned more and more with the beloved, bestows itself and wants to 'be there for' the other. The element of *agape* thus enters into this love, for otherwise *eros* is impoverished and even loses its own nature" (n. 7).

At the risk of coming off as a bit too academic, allow me to theologize for a moment. My hope is that this will allow us to see how the unity of erotic and divine love flows *from* the Trinity *through* Christ *to* the concrete lives of men and women.

Again, in the unity of *eros* and *agape* (human and divine love), we encounter the mystery of Christ and the unity of the human and divine natures within him. In turn, the perfect unity-in-distinction of the divine and human natures in Christ leads us back to the perfect unity-in-distinction of the three Persons in the one Trinitarian God. As there is one God, who is love, there is only "one reality of love," as Benedict observes. But just as there are different Persons united in God and two different natures united in Christ, so there are different aspects of love that form a unity-in-distinction.

The more the human dimension of love (*eros*) opens to the divine dimension of love (*agape*), the more we experience the true nature of love in its unity and integrity, that is, we experience love as it was meant to be from the very beginning. When *eros* refuses to open itself to the divine dimension of love—to that deep concern for the other, even to the point of laying down one's life—it "loses its own nature," as Benedict rightly asserts. The nature of *eros* is to lead man and woman to that total and irrevocable gift of self *to* and *for* the other, and *to* and *for* the offspring that might result from their mutual surrender. When *eros* is cut off from divine love, it is not concerned for the other (or for the offspring) but for itself and its own satisfaction. It does not want to bestow itself or "be there for" the other but to please itself, even if that means abandoning the other.

This tragic impoverishment of *eros* can never satisfy the longings of the human heart. But are men and women willing to pay the price of renunciation, sacrifice, and discipline required to find and live the love that *does* satisfy? The answer to this question will determine the entire course of a person's life.

30. Man "cannot always give, he must also receive. Anyone who wishes to give love must also receive love as a gift" (n. 7).

Receptivity is the fundamental posture of every creature before the Creator. We have nothing that we have not first received, beginning with our very existence. Love does not originate in us. It originates in God, who is love. Hence, if we are to give love, we must first open up to receive it. We cannot give what we do not have.

Before Christ gives us his new commandment to love as he has loved us, he first shows us the source of this love, the spring from which we can freely *receive* this love in order to *give* it to others: "As the Father has loved me, so have I loved you; abide in my love." Christ is the "Beloved" of the Father, the one whom the Father has loved eternally. Christ is able to show us the love of the Father only because he, from all eternity, has *received* it, abided in it. In turn, only after inviting us to abide in his love does Jesus command us to "love one another as I have loved you" (Jn 15:9, 12).

Whoever looks at the demands of the Gospel and concludes that he is not capable of living them is correct. At this point we either throw in the towel, water down the Gospel's demands, or cry out to God for the grace to do what we cannot do on our own. The first two options close us in on ourselves, effectively cutting us off from our full potential. The third option, the cry of the heart to God to supply what we lack, opens us up to faith and makes us receptive to the gift of divine love.

What makes the Gospel "good news" is that God supplies the grace for us to fulfill what he commands. It's not a matter of pulling ourselves up by our bootstraps and just "trying really hard" to love. Because of our fallen condition, we cannot do it. But when we are weak, then we are strong (see 2 Cor 12:10) because God offers us his own strength in our weakness. As John Paul II wrote, "To imitate and live out the love of Christ is not possible for man by his own strength alone. He becomes *capable of this love only by virtue of a gift received*" (*VS*, n. 22). "We love, because he first loved us" (1 Jn 4:19). We give love, because we have first received it from the God who is love.

We can almost feel St. Augustine's exuberance upon discovering this good news in his prayer, "Grant what you command and command what you will."

31. "Certainly, as the Lord tells us, one can become a source from which rivers of living water flow (cf. Jn 7:37-38). Yet to become such a source, one must constantly drink anew

from the original source, which is Jesus Christ, from whose pierced heart flows the love of God (cf. Jn 19:34)" (n. 7).

St. John is the one who reports that, when the soldier pierced Christ's side, "at once there came out blood and water" (Jn 19:34). He is also "the disciple whom Jesus loved, who had lain close to his breast at the supper" (Jn 21:20). What treasures were revealed to John as he lay there on Jesus' chest, listening to his beating heart? What exchange of human and divine love? The same perfection of love that John *felt* beating in Jesus' heart during the Last Supper he then *saw* the next day flowing from his opened side. As we shall see in what follows, this was the moment of John's "new birth."

Years ago, while listening to a recorded lecture of Bishop Fulton Sheen, my eyes were opened to new dimensions of the mystery of the cross. Sheen's booming voice still echoes in my mind: "Do you know what is happening at the foot of the cross?" he asked. "*Nuptials,* I tell you! *Nuptials!*" Describing the cross as a "marriage bed" mounted not in pleasure but in pain, the good bishop challenged his listeners to recognize the rich significance of Christ's words to Mary and John: "'Woman, behold, your son!' Then he said to the disciple, 'Behold, your mother!'" (Jn 19:26-27). Bishop Sheen went on to explain that whenever Jesus calls Mary "woman" (such as at the wedding in Cana and at the cross), He is speaking as the new Adam to the new Eve, the Bridegroom to the Bride. Here, of course, the relationship is outside the realm of blood. The fact that this "Bride" is Jesus' biological mother needn't trouble us. The marriage of the new Adam and new Eve consummated at the cross is mystical and virginal. The

Catechism refers to this "Woman" (Mary) as "the Bride of the Lamb" (*CCC*, n. 1138).

Penetrating these mystical realms opens up treasures for us "from which rivers of living water" flow, to use Benedict's expression. Just as the first Adam was put into a deep sleep and Eve came from his side, so the new Adam accepts the slumber of death and the new Eve—the Church, symbolized here by Mary—is born of his side in the flow of blood and water, which points to baptism and the Eucharist (see *CCC*, n. 766, 1067). The Church is betrothed to Christ in the "nuptial bath" of Baptism and their union consummated in the wedding feast of the Eucharist (see *CCC*, n. 1617). This great "nuptial mystery" is artistically portrayed by the renowned image of Mary holding a chalice (or sometimes a large jug reminiscent of Cana) at the foot of the cross receiving the flow of blood and water from Christ's side. And the union of the hearts of the new Adam and the new Eve ("A sword will pierce through your own soul also," Lk 2:35) has already borne supernatural fruit. At the foot of the cross, Jesus gives John a new mother and Mary a new son. Here the beloved disciple represents the offspring "born anew, not of perishable seed but of imperishable" (1 Pt 1:23), "not of blood...but of God" (Jn 1:13).

It is this new birth in the "living waters" of baptism and this redemptive blood which we "constantly drink anew" in the Eucharist that enable us to love as God loves: in a more and more perfect integration of *eros* and *agape*. The scene at the foot of the cross—the trinity of love between the new Adam, the new Eve, and the beloved disciple—presents, in fact, the perfect integration of *eros* and *agape*.

That heaving, sweating, bleeding body giving itself over, poured out so that we may live—that is the most perfect expression of love ever manifested on earth. It is the love we yearn for. And it is *ours*. We need only open to the gift. At the foot of the cross, Mary offers a perfect human openness. In Christ the gift is perfectly *given*. In Mary, it is perfectly *received*. The beloved disciple's "new birth" is the proof of it.

32. "In the account of Jacob's ladder, the Fathers of the Church saw this inseparable connection between ascending and descending love, between *eros* which seeks God and *agape* which passes on the gift received" (n. 7).

Eros is considered "ascending" love because it seeks, yearns, and searches for ecstasy, happiness, and transcendence. *Agape*, on the other hand, involves a divine "descending" to man in sacrifice and oblation. In the Old Testament, Jacob "dreamed that there was a ladder set up on the earth, and the top of it reached to heaven; and behold, the angels of God were ascending and descending on it!" (Gen 28:12). In the New Testament, Christ echoed these words: "Truly, truly, I say to you, you will see heaven opened, and the angels of God ascending and descending upon the Son of man" (Jn 1:51).

Christ is the ladder between heaven and earth. Christ comes down from heaven (*agape*) to fulfill all human yearning (*eros*). Christ is the "living water." If we drink it, we will never thirst again (see Jn 4:14). He is the living "bread of life." If we eat it, we will never hunger (see Jn 6:35). What a stunning proposal! To the degree that we experience this living hope of fulfillment in Christ, we long to pass on the gift we have received. In this reality of yearning, receiving, and passing on, we discover the integration of the sensual and the sacred, the sexual and the spiritual, the human and the divine, *eros* and *agape*.

Eros seeks a fulfillment that, in all reality, no human being can supply. God alone is the satisfaction of the heart's desire. Hence, God is the ultimate object of *eros*. At the root of all sexual yearning is really a cry for God. At the root of all desire we discover our thirst for infinity. St. Augustine said, "Our life is a gymnasium of desire... When we say 'God,' what do we wish to express? This word is all that we are waiting for" (*TJ* 4:2008-2009). We "wait" because we do not yet see and know God as he is. But even in the here and now, especially in and through the mystery of prayer and the sacraments, we can see, hear, feel, smell, and taste something of God. To the degree that we have received and live in this divine gift, we desire, in turn, to be the same gift to others that God has been to us. As Benedict says, *eros* "seeks God and *agape*...passes on the gift received."

33. **"Fundamentally, 'love' is a single reality, but with different dimensions." When *eros* and *agape* "are totally cut off from one another, the result is a caricature or at least an impoverished form of love" (n. 8).**

What does *eros* look like when we cut it off from *agape*? At first there is a certain sense of liberation. Loving as God loves requires internal restraint of lustful, self-serving impulses. Abdicating that responsibility removes what seems to many a heavy burden. But refusing the responsibility of disciplining and sublimating *eros* inevitably turns man in on himself. The meaning of one's sexuality shifts from other-focused to self-centered—from something "nuptial" to something "narcissistic." Rather than ending in "communion" with others (spouse and children), *eros* removed from *agape* ends in a "masturbatory self-absorption." One's attitude shifts from "serve others even at the expense of myself" to "serve myself even at the expense of others." And because sexuality "is by no means something purely biological, but concerns the innermost being of the human person" (*FC*, n. 11), a shift at such a fundamental level can slowly but surely change one's entire life paradigm from self-donation to self-gratification.

What does *agape* look like when we exclude *eros* from it? Again, at first there is a certain sense of liberation. A purely "spiritual" love (as if this were possible for man) is neat and clean, prim and proper, unencumbered by the messiness of the flesh. But cutting off *agape* from *eros* ultimately leaves us with a god who does not come to his creatures "in the flesh," a god who is ultimately nothing but an abstraction. Such a god is not the Christian God. A phantom deity is much more believable and—let's be honest—much more becoming than a God who wore diapers. A God who loves us in some abstract "spiritual" way is much more comfortable than a God who literally *bleeds* to love us and, what's more, invites us to drink his blood! (Even as I write this, I find it shocking.) And since the Incarnation (the marriage of divine and human love, *agape* and *eros*) is the distinction of Christian faith, a shift at such a fundamental level slowly but surely changes one's religion from Christianity to something heretically "other."

Much is at stake in our understanding of the relationship between *eros* and *agape*. When we cut them off from each other, we end not only with a caricature and impoverishment of love, but also with a caricature and impoverishment of our concept of God and of ourselves. If God is love, and if man can find himself only by learning to love, then our concept of love has a direct impact on our concept of God (theology) and our concept of man (anthropology). Christianity proposes a profound unity between God and man without, of course, blurring the distinction. This God-man unity (theological anthropology), resting on the Incarnation, is so profound that the Church does not hesitate to proclaim that "the Son of God became man so that we might become God" (*CCC*, n. 460). We could also put it this way: the Son of God experienced the human yearning of *eros*—"I thirst" (Jn 19:28)—so that we might experience the divine fire of *agape*—"I love!"

It is incorrect to consider *eros* "physical love" and *agape* "spiritual love." *Both* are spiritual realities with physical manifestations. The primary physical manifestation of *eros* is marital union, and the primary physical manifestation of *agape* is the Eucharist, the spousal union of Christ and the Church. Inasmuch as marital union and the Eucharist are interrelated (see Eph 5:21-32), so too are *eros* and *agape*. Only in this interrelationship of divine and human love do we understand who God is and who we are, because only in this interrelationship do we discover the one reality of love. Love, as Benedict says, is a single reality, but with different dimensions.

34. "Biblical faith does not set up a parallel universe, or one opposed to that primordial human phenomenon which is love, but rather accepts the whole man; it intervenes in his search for love in order to purify it and to reveal new dimensions of it" (n. 8).

When we follow Christ, nothing of our true humanity is destroyed, suppressed, or deleted. Rather, everything truly human is restored, redeemed, and completed. That's cause for great joy! Christ takes nothing of our authentic humanity away from us. It is the thief who comes to steal, kill, and destroy. Christ came to give us life and life to the full (see Jn 10:10).

Biblical faith intervenes in our search for love in order to guide it toward its true satisfaction. There are a million-and-one counterfeit loves on the market. They entice us incessantly and convincingly, promising happiness but delivering disappointment and even despair. How often have you heard that we must be in the world but not of it? Biblical faith does *not* command us to abandon our longings or to jump ship into a different, parallel universe. Biblical faith opens the human heart to the satisfaction of its yearnings through the redemption of *this* world. Christ did not come to condemn the world but to save it (see Jn 3:17). For God created this world and, upon seeing everything that he had made, proclaimed that it was "very good" (see Gen 1:31).

We flounder in this world only because we have lost sight of its original goodness and meaning. We needn't abandon this world to find that meaning or to find God. God meets us right here, literally coming to earth to redeem us and, with us, the earth. As we observed in chapter one, "God comes to us in the things we know best and can verify most easily, the things of our everyday life, apart from which we cannot understand ourselves" (*FR*, n. 12). What do we know better, what can we verify more easily, what is more everyday than our yearning for love? Apart from "that primordial human phenomenon which is love," apart from *eros*, "we cannot understand ourselves."

Christians often assert that "Jesus is the answer," but the answer to what? Jesus is the answer to that deep cry of the human heart for love. That cry of the heart that we've called *eros* is fulfilled only in union with Christ and his Church. That's the Christian proposal in a nutshell. When we allow biblical faith to purify the human search for love, we discover an entirely new dimension of satisfaction and fulfillment that is beyond our wildest imaginings. We discover, as St. Paul proposes, that "reason" for which God made us male and female and called us to become one flesh "from the beginning." As I wrote in my book *Theology of the Body Explained*,

> "For this reason...the two become one flesh." For what reason? To reveal, proclaim, and anticipate the union of Christ and the Church (see Eph 5:31-32). The eternal, ecstatic, "nuptial" Communion with Christ and the entire communion of saints—so far superior to anything proper to earthly life that we cannot begin to fathom it—this alone can satisfy the human "ache" of solitude. This is the North Pole to which that magnetic pull of erotic desire is oriented. And *this* is why "Jesus is

the answer." If the spirit of the Gospel is not *incarnated* as such, it will forever remain detached from what is essentially human. It will forever remain outside the scope of essentially human experiences. Yet, Christ took on flesh to wed himself indissolubly to that which is essentially human. Hence, if the Gospel is not incarnated with what is essentially human, it is essentially not the Gospel of Jesus Christ (*TBE,* p. 483).

Chapter 6

GOD'S *EROS*

35. "The divine power that Aristotle at the height of Greek philosophy sought to grasp...does not love: it is solely the object of love. The one God in whom Israel believes, on the other hand, loves with a personal love...and his love may certainly be called *eros*, yet it is also totally *agape*" (n. 9).

*P*hilosophy can know that God exists. It can even discern certain things about the divine power at the source of existence. But can we conclude without the aid of God's self-revelation (without biblical faith) that God loves? Aristotle could conclude only that the divine majesty is to be loved. He did not discern that the divine power not only loves but *is* love. Christ is the fullest revelation of this eternal truth. And Christ came as a Bridegroom to give up his body for his Bride, the Church, and for all humanity. Since the love of a bridegroom for his bride involves *eros*, Benedict affirms that God's love "may certainly be called *eros*."

This, it seems to me, is the most provocative assertion of Benedict's entire letter. In fact, as a reader of numerous papal documents, this is one of the boldest statements I've ever read from a pope. Never, to my knowledge, has a pope stated so plainly and certainly that God's love is not only *agape* but *eros*. For those familiar with the Bible's erotic imagery, this shouldn't come as a surprise. A widespread angelistic piety, however, is decidedly uncomfortable with such imagery. God loves with *eros!*? Is this not an affront to God? Shouldn't we recoil? Is this not somehow a degradation of his divinity, an entrapment of God's Spirit within the material world and a blasphemous projection of the human onto the divine? It could be, and would be, if it did not flow from a biblical vision of *eros* liberated from lust and from a deep well of respect and awe before the mystery of the Incarnation.

Herein lies the scandal of the Christian claim: God reveals his divine love through a human heart: the "sacred heart" of Jesus, the Christ, the God-Man. In other words, God reveals divine love through human love. It is only from "within" the logic of the Incarnation that Benedict can declare that God's "love may certainly be called *eros*." Yet, as he himself adds, pressing yet again into the unity of the divine and human natures in Christ without blurring the distinction, "it is also totally *agape*." This also marks the path of sanctification for Christian men and women: *eros*, through a progressive growth in holiness, must come more and more to express *agape*. And this is the path not only for spouses but for everyone, regardless of vocation. Everyone in the unity of body and soul as male or female is called to love as God loves, that is, with an *eros* that "is also totally *agape*."

It follows, then, that *eros* cannot be limited to its genital expression. *Eros* implies a yearning for all that is true, good, and beautiful, a yearning that cries out for expression. *Eros*, in this broad sense, shows itself in the pure delight a child takes in a flower, or in the passion of an artist or a poet. The Bible offers examples of *eros* not only in the Song of Songs but in the psalmist's repeated "shouts of joy" and in David's wild dancing before the Ark of the Covenant. The king, in fact, had so abandoned himself to *eros* that he scandalized Saul's daughter (see 2 Samuel 6:16-23). But there was no need for scandal, for this was an *eros* delighting in the Lord, an *eros* infused with *agape*.

36. "The Prophets, particularly Hosea and Ezekiel, described God's passion for his people using boldly erotic images" (n. 9).

The story of Hosea taking a prostitute for a wife at the Lord's command is well known. In this marriage we discover an image of God's love for us, his unfaithful spouse. God speaks through the Prophet of his *eros-agape* love for this unfaithful bride as follows:

> Therefore, behold, I will allure her, and bring her into the wilderness, and speak tenderly to her...And there she shall answer as in the days of her youth, as at the time when she came out of the land of Egypt. And in that day, says the LORD, you will call me, "My husband"... And I will espouse you for ever; I will espouse you in righteousness and in justice, in steadfast love, and in mercy. I will espouse you in faithfulness; and you shall know the LORD (Hos 2:14-20).

Betrothed love is the proper expression of *eros*. Yet, since this betrothal expresses God's love for his people, this *eros* "is also totally *agape*," as Benedict wrote. It is a love that yearns for intimacy with the "other" and rejoices in that other's beauty. "As the bridegroom rejoices over the bride, so shall your God rejoice over you" (Is 62:5).

The Prophet Ezekiel's imagery is even more explicit:

> And you grew up and became tall and arrived at full maidenhood; your breasts were formed, and your hair had grown; yet you were naked and bare. When I passed by you again and looked upon you, behold, you were at the age for love...I pledged myself to you and entered into a covenant with you, says the Lord GOD, and you became mine (Ez 16:7-8).

The internal difficulty we often encounter in allowing this erotic imagery to speak to us of God's holy love stems from what we might call "pornographic interference." We have been conditioned by our pornographic culture to think of the body and sexuality in a radically distorted way. When this distorted vision of the body appears as the "norm," it becomes increasingly difficult to reclaim the pure meaning of the body, sexuality, and erotic love. When we seek to do so, we are often overwhelmed by pornographic interference— like static snow on a TV screen. You try to make out the image, but interference distorts the picture.

Pope John Paul II taught that the body and erotic love have a "prophetic" meaning. The body "speaks." In the passionate union of spouses imbued by God with generative, creative power, the body proclaims a "great mystery"—the mystery of Trinitarian love revealed in Christ's union with the Church (see Eph 5:31-32). But wherever prophets are sent to proclaim truth, false prophets inevitably appear with cunning schemes to distort that truth and deceive God's people.

Pornographers are false prophets. And our failure as God's people to see the true *theological* meaning of the body and erotic love is a measure of their success. If we find it difficult or even impossible to see the mystery of God revealed through the human body and human sexuality, it may well be because we have been "evangelized" by men like Hugh Hefner and Larry Flynt, rather than by men like John Paul II and Benedict XVI. This is why our culture (beginning with the baptized themselves), as both popes have insisted, is desperately in need of a new evangelization.

37. True humanism "consists in the fact that man, through a life of fidelity to the one God, comes to experience himself as loved by God, and discovers joy in truth and in righteousness" (n. 9).

Secular humanism claims that man is capable of self-fulfillment without reference to God. It claims, in fact, that fidelity to God, especially the God of the Old and New Testaments, is the sure path to *de*humanization. In other words, Christian faith, the secular humanists claim, is the sure path to losing one's true humanity.

Contrast this with the Second Vatican Council's proclamation: "The truth is that only in the mystery of the incarnate Word does the mystery of man take on light. For Adam, the first man, was a figure of him who was to come, namely Christ the Lord. Christ, the final Adam, by the revelation of the mystery of the Father and his love, fully reveals man to man himself and makes his supreme calling clear" (*GS*, n. 22).

Whom should we believe, the secular humanists or the Fathers of the Second Vatican Council? Is Christ the sure path of man's authentic fulfillment and ennoblement, as the Council taught? Or is he the sure path of man's ignobleness, as the secular humanists teach? As Pope Paul VI said at the end of Vatican II, "Secular humanism... defied the Council." In the Council's teaching, the "religion of the God who became man has met the religion (for such it is) of man who makes himself God" (*CS*, n. 10).

Why does man make himself God? He does so because he is created for divine glory, but he doesn't believe in "the gift." He doesn't really believe God loves him, so he thinks he must grasp at divinity for himself if he is to attain it. The *Catechism* explains that "man was destined to be fully 'divinized' by God in glory. Seduced by the devil, he wanted to 'be like God,' but 'without God, before God, and not in accordance with God'" (*CCC*, n. 398).

If God is a tyrant with a desire to enslave us, then the secular humanists are entirely correct: man can fulfill himself only by liberating himself from the very idea of God. But is God a tyrant? Does Christ reveal the meaning of our humanity by asserting God's tyrannical rule? No! It's worth reviewing the above statement from the Council. This is the faith of the Catholic Church: Christ reveals the meaning of our humanity *by showing us the Father's love*. The crucified Christ is the ultimate rebuttal to the perennial lie that God jealously hoards his own glory. Christ emptied himself of glory so that we might be filled with it! "The glory which you [Father] have given me I have given to them" (Jn 17:22). Who do we think put that yearning for glory in our hearts in the first place? God put it there to lead us to a free act of faith in his love, in his *gift*. Blessed are they who believe (see Lk 1:45).

Thus, it is "through a life of fidelity to the one God" that man "comes to experience himself as loved by God," as Benedict says. In this self-giving divine love, man discovers his true self, his true identity. In this self-giving divine love, man discovers the path of an authentic humanism. The divine image in the human being reveals that "man, who is the only creature on earth which God willed for itself, cannot fully find himself except through a sincere gift of himself" (*GS*, n. 24). When man cuts himself off from God, he flounders in an isolated, "masturbatory" search for gratification. Other persons have value only insofar as one can derive pleasure from them. Such a person seeks joy in what *feels* good rather than in what *is* good. He seeks joy in transitory pleasures rather than "in truth and in righteousness," as the above quotation from Benedict states.

In this search for pleasure, we treat others not as persons created for *their* own sake but as things created for *our* own sake, to be used and maybe even discarded at whim. This is not humanism, but *de*humanism. Humanism leads to love, and love comes from God. Hence, there can be no true humanism apart from a fruitful union of love between God and man.

38. "God's *eros* for man is also totally *agape*. This is not only because it is bestowed in a completely gratuitous manner, without any previous merit, but also because it is love which forgives" (n. 10).

There are here two essential and interrelated points on which to reflect. First, God's *eros-agape* love is bestowed without any previous merit. Second, God's *eros-agape* love is a love that forgives. We are all guilty of "playing the harlot" in relationship to God. The prophet Hosea's message is that *God forgives our adultery and prostitution*. God's love is a love we simply do not and *cannot* earn. We all stand as sinners before God. But forgiveness "bears witness that, in our world, love is stronger than sin" (*CCC*, n. 2844).

God's love is entirely *gratuitous*, and God's love *forgives*. We've heard this before, but my guess is that few of us really believe it. In my experience speaking to Catholic audiences around the world, it seems that many of us are still trying futilely to earn God's love. "Good boys and girls go to heaven; bad boys and girls don't; so you'd better be a good boy or girl." Many a Catholic has grown up with this kind of message as a basic framework for "reaching heaven," even though this is *not* what the Church truly teaches or believes. As a result, we often believe that a scale weighing our good works against our sins will determine our eternal destiny. If this is the case, we simply can't afford to admit the depth of sin in our lives; the implications are too devastating. So we rationalize our sin and continue to comfort ourselves by recalling that we're not nearly as bad as "those really nasty sinners down the street."

But where is the death and resurrection of Jesus in this view of salvation? If we are convinced God loves us and we're going to heaven because, well, "I'm a good person," what do we need a savior for? "God shows his love for us in that while we were yet sinners Christ died for us" (Rom 5:8).

To counter this notion of salvation on the tipping scale, a wise retreat master once proposed the following image of "Judgment Day." Each of us will be on trial before God the Father, he said. The prosecuting attorney, the devil, will be listing all our sins one by one. All those things the deceiver convinced us were good in this life he will now throw in our faces as evidence against us, snarling with certainty, "Guilty...guilty...guilty." Knowing we are indeed guilty, we will have no defense, unless...unless in this life we have abandoned ourselves entirely to Christ and his mercy. If we have, every time the devil snarls, "Guilty...guilty...guilty," Christ will display his own wounds to the Father and proclaim, "Forgiven... forgiven...forgiven."

People are afraid of sin because they are afraid of condemnation. However, there is "no condemnation for those who are in Christ Jesus" (Rom 8:1). We needn't fear to admit the depth of our sin so long as we never talk about it, think about it, or otherwise acknowledge it outside the context of its divine antidote: *mercy*. God loves us not in spite of the misery of our sin. It is our misery, in fact, as Father Jean d'Elbée observes in his marvelous book *I Believe in Love*, that attracts God's mercy. Recall, as we said earlier, that mercy in Latin, *misericordia*, actually means "a heart which gives itself to those in misery."

There is only one lasting misery, only one unforgivable sin. Christ called it blaspheming the Holy Spirit (see Mt 12:31). In the sacrament of reconciliation, when the priest absolves us, he reminds us that the Holy Spirit was sent for the forgiveness of sins. To "blaspheme" the Holy Spirit, then, is to reject God's mercy. "There are no limits to the mercy of God, but anyone who deliberately refuses to accept his mercy...rejects the forgiveness of his sins and the salvation offered by the Holy Spirit. Such hardness of heart can lead to final impenitence and eternal loss" (*CCC*, n. 1864).

Thus, we needn't fear admitting our sins, though they be horrid and many. We need only fear rationalizing our sins. By doing so, we freely place ourselves outside God's providence for our sins. That providence is the saving work of Jesus' death and resurrection. "If we say we have no sin, we deceive ourselves. ...If we confess our sins, he...will forgive our sins and cleanse us from all unrighteousness" (I Jn 1:8-9). This is the unfathomable glory of God's *eros-agape* love. Let us repent and believe in the good news!

39. "God's passionate love for his people—for humanity—is at the same time a forgiving love. It is so great that it turns God against himself, his love against his justice" (n. 10).

Is it just *just* to be just? Or, in fact, does justice include and even demand love? If justice demands love, then justice already "contains" forgiveness, so to speak. For love—to the degree that it participates in that divine *eros-agape*—is so great that it compels us to forgive. Christ, in fact, commands us to do so: "Be merciful, even as your Father is merciful" (Lk 6:36). Even more—"and this is daunting," admits the *Catechism*—God's "mercy cannot penetrate our hearts as long as we have not forgiven those who have trespassed against us" (*CCC*, n. 2840).

If the love of man and woman is to flourish, it *must* be a love that forgives. What a dangerous prospect it is to put a fallen man and a fallen woman into a house together and say "work it out" until death do you part! The fallen nature of men and women almost sets them up for a "perfect storm." Without large and continual doses of mercy and forgiveness, the male-female relationship is doomed from the start.

Forgiveness, however, is often misunderstood. It does not mean saying "It's okay" to someone who has wounded you. If it were "okay," there would be no reason to forgive the person. Furthermore, forgiveness does not remove the offender's responsibility before God or, if applicable, before the civil law. Rather, forgiving someone means releasing that person to God's justice and mercy. It means allowing God's love (the Holy Spirit) to penetrate and permeate our wounded hearts and, through that, allowing God's love to reach the heart of the person who has wounded us. As the *Catechism* wisely observes, "It is not in our power not to feel or to forget an offense; but the heart that offers itself to the Holy Spirit turns injury into compassion and purifies the memory in transforming the hurt into intercession" (*CCC*, n. 2843).

The hurt that the sins of others cause us is real. But, if we have the courage to allow the miracle of mercy to work in us, that hurt can be transformed into prayer, into intercession. Sin committed against us can become—if we allow it—an occasion of salvation, both for us and for the person who sinned against us. We pray that God would forgive us our trespasses *as* we forgive those who trespass against us. "This crucial requirement...is impossible for man. But 'with God all things are possible'" (*CCC*, n. 2841).

40. "So great is God's love for man that by becoming man he follows him even into death, and so reconciles justice and love" (n. 10).

Allow me to tell an inspiring family story that illustrates the reconciliation of justice and love. My son John Paul, although young, has a deep love for the Lord. One of his joys in turning seven was knowing that he would soon receive Jesus in the Eucharist. Not long after his First Communion, I was heading off to our local parish's 9:00 a.m. daily Mass. At 8:35 I came down the steps and found John Paul just finishing his breakfast. "Too bad, buddy," I said. "I wanted to take you to Mass, but you missed the hour fast before Communion." Daily Mass in our small country parish lasts only about twenty minutes. By 9:35 we would have been another twenty minutes past the time of receiving Communion.

John Paul was beside himself. "I can't go to Mass and not receive Jesus. I just can't!" Wanting to meet his desire, I said, "You know what? I bet if I explain to Father Moratelli that you didn't know I would be taking you to Mass today, he'll grant you a dispensation from the fast." I explained what that meant, and we headed off to Mass a few minutes early to speak to Father, both of us confident he would understand.

To my surprise and John Paul's dismay, Father Moratelli didn't think the situation warranted a dispensation. I pleaded my case with a look in my eyes that said, "Father, you don't understand what I'm going to have to deal with if my son can't receive Jesus." When he looked at John Paul, he saw clearly how disappointed he was. "Gosh, John Paul, what am I supposed to do?" he asked with befuddlement. "Now you're going to be mad at me and mad at the Church. I don't make up the rules, but"—I was convinced (and selfishly delighted) that he was about to grant the dispensationn—"I really believe we need to respect them." No luck! He was sticking to his guns.

Such decisions are a matter of a priest's prudential judgment, which I knew we needed to respect. Still, I must admit, I was a bit miffed. My young son was longing to receive Jesus. He acted in ignorance when he ate his breakfast. Father *could* have granted a dispensation but wouldn't. Obviously none of this is a big deal in the objective scheme of things. But in that moment, to my son, this *was* a big deal. As his father, I was concerned for his heart and wondered how all of this was going to turn out. I was sure there had to be a lesson in it for him somewhere. I tried to encourage him to trust that Father Moratelli wanted what was best for him.

Mass began as usual. But after Father read the Gospel, nothing was usual. He gave a long homily. He never does that at a daily Mass. During the Eucharistic prayer he was adding all these unusual silent pauses. Only then did it dawn on me what was going on. A lump seized my throat and tears welled up in my eyes. As communion time approached, John Paul was still wrestling with his disappointment, unaware of what was happening. During the kiss of peace, Father Moratelli came out to shake hands with everyone in the congregation. He *never* does that. He came to John Paul last and with a big, loving grin on his face said, "John Paul, peace be with you." Then he whispered, "In one minute it will be nine-thirty... *five.*" As the significance of that statement dawned on John Paul, his sorrow vanished and a look of wonder and delight beamed on his face.

Benedict tells us that God's love for man is so great that "he follows him even into death, and so reconciles justice and love." That day Father Moratelli followed my son into his own suffering and reconciled justice and love. Truth and mercy kissed (see Ps 85:10). In the car on the way home, I said to John Paul, "Father Moratelli taught you a beautiful lesson today. How would you sum it up?" Having recently watched *The Sound of Music*, John Paul replied, "Well, whenever God closes a door, he always opens a window." "Yeah, bud, he sure does."

> 41. "The philosophical dimension to be noted in this biblical vision...lies in the fact that...God is the absolute and ultimate source of all being; but this universal principle of creation—the *Logos*, primordial reason—is at the same time a lover with all the passion of a true love. *Eros* is thus supremely ennobled, yet at the same time it is so purified as to become one with *agape*" (n. 10).

The "*Logos*"—the logic at the source of all that exists—is not just some impersonal power of creation. This is about the best that a philosophical reflection can offer in its search for God. Divine revelation, since it comes from God himself, goes further, much further. In Christ we discover that the *Logos* is an eternal Person who loves with an eternal love. The *Logos* is "a lover with all the passion of a true love," as Benedict says. But there's still more. In Christ, the love and logic at the source of all that exists *was made flesh*. Jesus of Nazareth is the *Logos* made flesh! This divine Person, as we observed previously, loves with a human heart. "*Eros* is thus supremely ennobled, yet at the same time it is so purified as to become one with *agape*."

To help us reflect on these truths, I'd like to turn to what may seem an unlikely source: Bono, lead singer of U2, one of the biggest rock bands in the world. In a book-long interview with music journalist Michka Assayas, Bono reflects at length on his religious convictions. Assayas simply cannot understand how the world's biggest rock star could believe that Jesus is the Son of God. Nor can he understand how Bono has remained faithful to his wife of twenty-five years. In the portions of dialogue that follow, Bono, in a stroke of genius, turns his baffled interviewer's suggestion of "incarnating" lustful temptations on its head by reflecting on the relationship between *eros*, *agape*, and his belief in the Incarnation of God's Son.

> *Assayas:*   But you're the singer and front man in a band, and it's not just any band. I'm sure you've been tempted. Don't you ever feel that no matter what you have decided [about fidelity to your wife], love needs to be incarnated? . . . Think of *groupies*.
>
> *Bono:*   We never fostered that environment. If you mean *groupie* in the sense that I know it, which is sexual favors traded for proximity with the band. . . Taking advantage of a fan, sexual bullying is to be avoided,

but the music is sexual. ....Sometimes...the erotic
love [we sing about] can turn into something much
higher, and bigger notions of love, and God, and
family. It seems to segue very easily for me between
those.

Assayas: I'm surprised at how easily religion comes up
in your answers, whatever the question is. How
come you're always quoting from the Bible? Was it
because it was taught at school? Or because your
father or mother wanted you to read it?

Bono: Let me try to explain something to you, which I
hope will make sense of the whole conversation...I
remember coming back from a very long tour...
Dublin at Christmas is cold, but it's lit up, it's like
Carnival in the cold. On Christmas Eve I went
to St. Patrick's Cathedral...It had dawned on me
before, but it really sank in: the Christmas story.
The idea that God, if there is a force of Love and
Logic in the universe, that it would seek to explain
itself is amazing enough. That it would seek to
explain itself and describe itself by becoming a
child born in straw poverty, in shit and straw,
a child, I just thought: "Wow!" Just the poetry.
Unknowable love, unknowable power, describes
itself as the most vulnerable. There it was. I was
sitting there, and...tears came down my face, and
I saw the genius of this, utter genius of picking a
particular point in time and deciding to turn on
this. Because that's exactly what we were talking
about earlier: love needs to find form, intimacy
needs to be whispered. To me, it makes sense.
It's actually logical. It's pure logic. Essence has to
manifest itself. It's inevitable. Love has to become
an action or something concrete. It would have

to happen. There must be an incarnation. Love
must be made flesh. Wasn't that your point earlier?
(*BMA*, pp. 119-120, 124-125)

This is a great example of how we can meet people right where
they are, receiving their understandable questions as an opportunity
to share the reasons for our faith. Michka Assayas is probably not at
a point where he can hear these truths coming from Pope Benedict.
But Bono, in his own way, makes the same points. What Benedict
calls "the Logos, primordial reason" Bono calls the "force of Love
and Logic in the universe." Benedict insists that this "Logos" is "a
lover with all the passion of a true love," while Bono expresses awe
for the passion of this lover who manifested himself in a manure-
ridden stable in Bethlehem. Benedict speaks of how *eros* is "supremely
ennobled" by *agape*, while Bono shares how erotic love segues very
easily for him into "higher and bigger notions of love, and God,
and family." A pope, a rock star, and a skeptical journalist might
speak different languages, but we can see that the same questions
about love and God find an echo in one way or another in every
human heart. We all yearn for love "to find form," as Bono put it,
for intimacy "to be whispered."

42. "The reception of the Song of Songs in the canon of
sacred Scripture was soon explained by the idea that these
love songs ultimately describe God's relation to man and
man's relation to God. Thus the Song of Songs became,
both in Christian and Jewish literature, a source of mystical
knowledge and experience, an expression of the essence of
biblical faith: that man can indeed enter into union with
God—his primordial aspiration" (n. 10).

Why is it that so many of the greatest mystics of Christian history
are inevitably drawn to an explicitly erotic love poem as their favorite
book in the Bible? It is because this erotic love poetry, as Pope Benedict
says, expresses "the essence of biblical faith"! We should let this truth
wash away all notions that the Church is opposed to sex or otherwise
views it negatively. Sexual love, as God intended it, offers us an analogy
that *takes us to the heart of biblical faith*. The union in one flesh expresses "that
man can indeed enter into union with God." This, from beginning to
end, is the central message and invitation of the Scriptures. And, from
beginning to end, the Bible presents the union of spouses as the primary
image by which we can comprehend and enter into this mystery of union
with God.

"'For this reason a man shall leave his father and mother and be
joined to his wife, and the two shall become one flesh.' This is a great
mystery, and I mean in reference to Christ and the Church" (Eph
5:31-32). This "magnificent synthesis concerning the 'great mystery'
appears," according to John Paul II, "as the compendium or *summa*,
in some sense, *of the teaching about God and man* which was brought to
fulfillment by Christ" (*LF*, n. 19). In this biblical comparison of
Christ's union with the Church to the one-flesh union of spouses,
we must recognize, as John Paul II also observed, that it "is not
only a comparison in the sense of a metaphor" (*TOB* 98:8). One
"must admit that the very essence of marriage contains *a particle of the
[divine] mystery*. Otherwise, this whole analogy would hang in a void"
(*TOB* 90:5). Thus, the "analogy of conjugal or spousal love helps us
penetrate into the very essence of the mystery" (*TOB* 95b:1).

The "essence" of the mystery is precisely union with God. As a sacrament, marriage not only symbolizes union with God; it really and truly brings it about. To the degree that they integrate *eros* and *agape*, spouses *are* living in union with God. "This seems to be *the integral meaning of the sacramental sign of marriage.* In this way, through the 'language of the body,' man and woman encounter the great *'mystery'*" (*TOB* 117b:6). They encounter the mystery of God's passionate *eros-agape* love consummated in Christ's union with his Bride, the Church. It is this love that the Church feels compelled to proclaim to the ends of the earth. All of her moral teachings are meant to ensure that this love shines forth. They are given to help men and women distinguish true love from its counterfeits. They are given to steer us away from the cheap wine and lead us toward the new wine of Cana.

Chapter 7

THE PURPOSE OF *EROS*

43. In the biblical narrative of creation, "the idea is certainly present that man is somehow incomplete, driven by nature to seek in another the part that can make him whole, the idea that only in communion with the opposite sex can he become 'complete.' The biblical account thus concludes with a prophecy about Adam: 'Therefore a man leaves his father and his mother and cleaves to his wife and they become one flesh' (Gen 2:24)" (n. 11).

*T*his "prophecy about Adam" is even more so a prophecy about the new Adam, Jesus Christ. If we have referenced St. Paul's words in Ephesians 5 once, we have done so a dozen times. But since they summarize the entire Bible, we *must* return to these words again and again to enter ever more deeply into the "great mystery."

Man's leaving father and mother to become one flesh with his bride refers to Christ and the Church. Let's be more specific. Christ is the one who left his Father in heaven; he left the home of his mother on earth, to give up his body for his Bride, so that we, the Bride of Christ, might become one-flesh with him. Where do we become one-flesh with Christ? We do so most fully here on earth in the Eucharist, which John Paul II described as the *"Sacrament of the Bridegroom and of the Bride."* Here, Christ is united with "the Church, his...'body' as the bridegroom with the bride. All this is contained in the Letter to the Ephesians." Even more, John Paul II continued, "Christ, in instituting the Eucharist...thereby wished to express the relationship between man and woman, between what is 'feminine' and what is 'masculine.' It is a relationship willed by God both in the mystery of creation and in the mystery of Redemption" (*MD*, n. 26).

In the mystery of creation, what is "masculine" and what is "feminine" is consummated in man and woman's becoming one flesh. In the mystery of Redemption, what is "masculine" and what is "feminine" is consummated in Christ and the Church's becoming one flesh. *Eros*, then—that burning desire for communion that God planted in our being on the day of creation—is meant to lead to *agape*—that fulfillment of communion that God offered us on the day of redemption. Perhaps we could say that *eros* is more specifically the love of creation and *agape* is more specifically the love of redemption. But let us not forget that *eros* and *agape* express different dimensions of the one mystery of love; they must never be dis-integrated. So, too, creation and redemption express different dimensions of the one mystery of God's love; they can never be dis-integrated (see *CCC*, n. 280).

The holy communion of creation (*eros*-marriage) is meant to lead us to the Holy Communion of redemption (*agape*-Eucharist). An integral look at that classic text of Ephesians 5, then, reveals that Christ is the satisfaction of all human yearning for communion! Christ is the end, the goal, the terminus, the consummation of *eros*. Everything that Benedict attributes to the longing for completeness between man and woman in the book of Genesis can be attributed to the human being in relation to Christ. Man "is somehow incomplete, driven by nature to seek in another [to seek in Christ] the part that can make him whole, the idea that only in communion with the opposite sex [only in Communion with Christ] can he become 'complete.' The biblical account thus concludes with a prophecy about Adam: 'Therefore a man leaves his father and his mother and cleaves to his wife and they become one flesh' (Gen 2:24)." It is a prophecy that the "ache" of man's solitude will be fulfilled beyond his wildest imaginings in the one-flesh unity of Christ and the Church.

44. "*Eros* is somehow rooted in man's very nature; Adam is a seeker, who 'abandons his mother and father' in order to find woman" (n. 11).

Have you ever seen the movie *The Truman Show*? It's not only worth watching; it's worth studying very closely. It offers an amazingly insightful look at "Adam's" nature as a seeker—a seeker of truth— and the internal and external obstacles we all encounter on the journey. The main character ("True-man") abandons everything in his search for the truth. Just as Benedict says, Truman "'abandons his mother and father' in order to find woman." In this case, her name is Sylvia.

Truman, the first baby to be legally adopted by a corporation, is raised in an enormous movie studio, a false enclosed island called Seahaven. There is a fake town with a fake bay, fake weather, a fake sun and moon, etc. Everyone in this false world is an actor except Truman (although, according to Truman's "best friend," Marlon,

"Nothing is fake; it's merely controlled"). Five thousand cameras hidden throughout the town capture Truman's every move, allowing the rest of the world to watch the ultimate "reality TV show" broadcast live twenty-four hours a day.

An interviewer asks the creator of the show, a sly, power-hungry antichrist figure named Christof ("Christ-off"), why Truman has never realized the false nature of his world. Christof responds, "We accept the reality of the world with which we're presented; it's as simple as that." But the "reality" with which Truman is presented doesn't always add up. In one of the opening scenes of the movie, Truman sees a stage light fall from the sky and crash onto the street. Puzzled, he gets in his car and drives to work, only to have the radio explain away his questions: "News flash just in: An aircraft in trouble began shedding parts as it flew over Seahaven."

Truman's questions, hopes, dreams, and sense of adventure are always squashed. When, as a schoolboy, he excitedly expresses a desire to be an explorer, his teacher pulls down a map and responds, "You're too late. There's nothing left to explore." As an adult, he longs to go to Fiji, but whenever his adventurous spirit presents itself, either his wife distracts him with an invitation to the bedroom or Marlon suddenly shows up with a six pack. Here we see examples of what Peter Kreeft explains in his book *How to Win the Culture War*. Satan's essential task, he says, "is not just to block the finding but to block the seeking. ...Eventually seekers find. So it is a vastly more efficient expenditure of energy to attack the seeking" (*HW*, pp. 69, 72). As Christof knows, numbing people with booze and sex is a great way to do it.

But the human being's desire for truth is ultimately indomitable. Even Christof admits, "If [Truman's] was more than just a vague ambition, if he was absolutely determined to discover the truth, there's no way we could prevent him." Truman's yearning for truth is indeed more than just a vague ambition. And the thing that keeps him searching is the memory of a woman who loved him.

In a flashback, Truman, as a college student, meets Sylvia, an actor with a script to follow like everyone else. Against Christof's wishes, she comes to love Truman. Love, if it is true, speaks truth. Knowing Christof's troopers will immediately sweep her away and take her off the show and out of Truman's life forever, she quickly tries to explain to Truman that his world is false and that the real world is watching him. Her "father" immediately shows up, pushes her into his car, and tells Truman he'll never see her again. "We're moving to Fiji," he insists. Sylvia breaks through the commotion of his lies, locks eyes with Truman, and says, "Come and find me!"

Eros, rightly directed, is a force to be reckoned with. It's what compels a person to seek the truth, and Christof knows it. As we've already seen, throughout Truman's life Christof has had to squelch or disorient Truman's yearnings (*eros*) to keep him on the fake island. Christof's biggest weapon is fear. When Truman was a boy, Christof staged the death of his father, having Truman witness his drowning in a mock sailing accident on the bay. Ever since, Truman has experienced a crippling hydrophobia. As an adult, he knows the answers to his questions can come only by his sailing headlong into his deepest fear. Somehow he knows he will discover "the truth" on the other side of the bay. So he courageously sets sail. At one point we catch a glimpse of the name of the boat: "Santa Maria."

Christof sends a storm, certain that Truman will turn back in fear. Truman, fighting to keep afloat, realizes that some mysterious force is actively seeking to thwart him. He ties himself to the boat and, with his body cruciform, cries out, *"Is that the best you can do!? You're gonna have to kill me!"* The message is clear: we must prefer death over ceasing our quest; we must set our hand to the plow and never look back (see Lk 9:62); only then are we capable of finding the truth.

Christof rages when he sees Truman's determination. In a last-ditch, power-mad attempt to stop him, he sends the mother of all waves to capsize the boat. Truman symbolically dies and then rises. The storm ceases. The waters become calm. The sun comes out from behind the clouds. The boat uprights itself. Truman raises his tattered sail and sails on. He soon crashes into the wall of the studio and stares the truth in the face.

In this poignant scene, Truman, overwhelmed with emotion, reaches out cautiously and curiously to touch the wall. Realizing that *everything* behind him has been a lie, realizing that his whole life has been a deception, he pounds the wall and collapses in tears. A few moments later he discovers a door marked "Exit" ("exodus" comes to mind) and pushes it open. Then Truman hears Christof's booming voice over the loud speaker:

Truman: Who are you?
Christof: I am the creator...of a television show.
Truman: Then who am I?

Christof:	You're the star.
Truman:	Was nothing real?
Christof:	You were real. ...Listen to me, Truman. There's no more truth out there than there is in the world I created for you. The same lies, the same deceit—but in my world, you have nothing to fear. I know you better than you know yourself.
Truman:	*You never had a camera in my head!*
Christof:	You're afraid; that's why you can't leave. I've been watching you your whole life...You can't leave, Truman.
Sylvia [watching on TV]:	Please, God! You can do it.
Christof:	You belong here with me.

Truman weighs his options. Everything behind him is false, to be sure, but it's familiar. It's the only world he's known. Everything through that door is real, to be sure, but it's totally unknown. Truman takes his final bow, and walks through the door. Sylvia, who has been waiting in the wings, rejoices and runs to greet him.

"*Eros* is somehow rooted in man's very nature; Adam is a seeker." Christ assures us, "Seek, and you will find" (Lk 11:9). Strap yourself to the ship. Face your deepest fears. Follow *eros* to the depths. You will discover the truth, "and the truth will make you free" (Jn 8:32).

45. "*Eros* directs man towards marriage, to a bond which is unique and definitive; thus, and only thus, does it fulfill its deepest purpose" (n. 11).

What is the deepest purpose of *eros*? It is not only to direct men and women toward marriage, for marriage is meant to direct men and women toward Christ and his love for the Church. Thus, we can recognize that the *deepest* purpose of *eros*—the reason God gave us a yearning for sexual union in the first place—is to point us to the eternal union of Christ and the Church. It has the capacity to do so, however, only to the degree that *eros* truly images and participates in Christ's love for the Church, that is, to the degree that *eros* is inspired by and integrated with *agape*.

Christ's love is not a compulsive response to an urge. Christ loves the Church freely ("No one takes [my life] from me, but I lay it down of my own accord," Jn 10:18). Christ's love has no safety nets, no back doors, no half measures, no escape clauses. Christ loves the Church without reservation ("he loved them to the end," Jn 13:1). Christ's love is not a one-night stand, here today and gone tomorrow. Christ loves the Church faithfully ("I am with you always," Mt 28:20). And Christ's love is not sterilely turned in on itself. Christ loves the Church fruitfully, that is, with the goal of expanding the circle of communion ("Go therefore and make disciples of all nations," Mt 28:19) and bearing forth life ("I came that they may have life, and have it abundantly," Jn 10:10).

This free, total, faithful, and fruitful self-giving is what erotic love is *meant* to express. Another name for this kind of love is *marriage*. Free, total, faithful, fruitful love, in fact, is precisely what a man and woman commit to at the altar. The priest or deacon asks them: "Have you come here *freely* and *without reservation* to give yourselves to each other in marriage? Do you promise to be *faithful* until death? Do you promise to *receive children* lovingly from God?" They answer yes. That yes is the richest affirmation of *eros* in its integral relationship with *agape*. Throughout their lives, spouses are to be faithful witnesses to the world of this integral relationship between *eros* and *agape*. In the ins and outs, ups and downs, good times and bad of married life, spouses are to continue offering that yes, that affirmation, that amen to the beauty and goodness of being created male and female in the image of God, who himself lives an eternal exchange of life-giving love.

When erotic love is cut off from *agape*, however, *eros* fails even to recognize itself. It doesn't understand or realize its orientation "towards marriage, to a bond which is unique and definitive," as Benedict says. In fact, a disintegrated *eros* comes to see marriage as an obstacle to its own fulfillment, an impediment to its unrestrained indulgence. How often do we hear marriage called "a ball and chain"? When we indulge *eros* without restraint, as we have already seen, we don't find the happiness we expected to find. "The alternative is clear: either man governs his passions and finds peace, or he lets himself be dominated by them and becomes unhappy" (*CCC*, n. 2339). Governing *eros* means overcoming the tyranny of our fallen passions, liberating the heart to seek what it truly desires at its deepest level: a love that lasts forever. Governing *eros* frees us to offer and experience such a love and never to settle for anything less.

46. "Corresponding to the image of a monotheistic God is monogamous marriage" (n. 11).

Since marriage is a "great mystery" that refers to Christ and the Church, the way we conceive of marriage has a direct impact on the way we conceive of Christ and the Church. Change our understanding of marriage, and we change our understanding of Christ and the

Church, of God and his love for us. Conversely, our concept of God and his love for us has a direct bearing on our understanding of marriage. Believing in one God (monotheism) logically leads to and calls for loving one spouse (monogamy).

There is one God who lives a unity-in-distinction among three Divine Persons. This one God, in the Person of Christ, has one Bride, one Church made up of a great multitude of persons who live (or are meant to live) a unity-in-distinction (see *CCC*, n. 813-814). To call the Church "catholic" is to recognize that it is universal. "Catholic" means universal, and universal means a oneness ("uni") among many ("versa"). When the followers of Christ fail to live in unity, that is, when they fail in "catholicity," in a sense they make of Christ a polygamist. This is the scandal of having thousands of Christian denominations. It appears that Christ has thousands of brides. Or, rather, the one Bride has been shattered into thousands of pieces.

Before speaking of the "great mystery" of spouses joining in one flesh, St. Paul begs Christ's followers to be "eager to maintain the unity of the Spirit in the bond of peace. There is one body and one Spirit...one Lord, one faith, one baptism, one God and Father of us all" (Eph 4:3-6). There is one Church (one Bride) precisely because there is one God (one Bridegroom). Christ's fidelity to his Bride flows from the fidelity of love within the Trinity. If spousal love flows from Christ, it leads to one spouse, one bond, one union, one marriage.

47. "Marriage based on exclusive and definitive love becomes the icon of the relationship between God and his people and vice versa. God's way of loving becomes the measure of human love" (n. 11).

Again, John Paul II's teaching can help illuminate Benedict's point. The spousal analogy "works in two directions," John Paul wrote. It allows us "to understand better the relationship of Christ with the Church" and it permits us "to penetrate more deeply into the essence of...marriage." In fact, "at the basis of the understanding of marriage in its very essence stands Christ's spousal relationship with the Church." In turn, marriage "becomes a *visible sign of the eternal divine mystery*, according to the image of the Church united with Christ. In this way, Ephesians leads us to *the very foundations of the sacramentality of marriage*" (*TOB* 90:4). Marriage is a sacrament that reveals Christ's love for the Church, and Christ's love for the Church is the ultimate reality that demonstrates the meaning and orientation of marriage as a sacrament. They point to each other.

In this invitation to spouses to participate in Christ's love for the Church, we discover, as Benedict says, that "God's way of loving becomes the measure of human love." This is a difficult love. No one can live it on his or her own. But we are not on our own. "God's love has been poured into our hearts through the Holy Spirit who has been given to us" (Rom 5:5). It is only in and through the power coming from the Holy Spirit that men and women are able to live *eros* in its fullest, most beautiful dimensions. The Church's sexual ethic begins to make sense when viewed through this lens. It is not a prudish list of prohibitions. It is a call to embrace our own "greatness," our own godlike dignity. It is a call to live the love we are created for—a call to experience the integration of *eros* and *agape* and to enjoy the abundant joys that come from this integration.

If sexual intercourse is meant to express the language of *agape*, then it is meant to express that free, total, faithful, and fruitful gift of self discussed above. In other words, sexual intercourse, if it is to be an honest expression of *eros-agape* love, must express the marriage commitment itself. Sexual union *incarnates* marital love, or, at least, it is *meant* to do so. It is meant to be that embrace in which the words of the wedding vows "become flesh." Ultimately, all questions of sexual morality come down to one simple question: Does this participate in God's *free, total, faithful,* and *fruitful* love, or does it not? If it does not, we should not settle for it. It will never correspond to the heart's yearning and will never bring that steadfast happiness for which we yearn.

Chapter 8

UNION AND EUCHARIST

48. "The ancient world had dimly perceived that man's real food—what truly nourishes him as man—is ultimately the *Logos*, eternal wisdom: this same *Logos* now truly becomes food for us—as love" (n. 13).

*T*he philosophers of the ancient world remotely sensed that to reach one's source—the wisdom, the ultimate reason behind man's existence, the "*Logos*"—was the path to human fulfillment, the true "nourishment" of man's being. Still, as indicated by the altar "to an unknown god" in Athens, the ancient philosophers sought this God "in the hope that they might feel after him and find him" (Acts 17:27), but they could not reach him; they did not know him. Paul, standing in the middle of the Areopagus in Athens, audaciously proclaims to the seekers that he knows this unknown God. He assures them that this *Logos* "is not far from each one of us, for 'In him we live and move and have our being'; as even some of your poets have said, 'For we are indeed his offspring'" (Acts 17:27-28).

This *Logos*, in fact, is closer to us than the ancient world could ever have imagined. In the fullness of time, the *Logos* for which man has reached, reached for man. In the fullness of time, this *Logos* actually became a man, born of a woman (see Gal 4:4). And, as Benedict says,

"This same *Logos* now truly becomes food for us." "O taste and see that the LORD is good!" (Ps 34:8). In the Old Testament, this idea of "tasting" the Lord's goodness was merely a metaphor. In the New Testament, the Lord's goodness becomes *real* food and *real* drink (see Jn 6:55). If we eat this food and drink this cup, we "will live for ever" (Jn 6:51).

> **49. In and through the Eucharist, the "imagery of marriage between God and Israel is now realized in a way previously inconceivable: it had meant standing in God's presence, but now it becomes union with God through sharing in Jesus' self-gift, sharing in his body and blood" (n. 13).**

John Paul II wrote that in the Old Testament the mystery expressed by the spousal analogy "is barely outlined, 'half open,' as it were; in Ephesians, by contrast, it is fully unveiled (without ceasing to be a mystery, of course)" (*TOB* 95:7). What is fully unveiled? In Christ, we are called to *union*—Holy Communion—with God, who himself lives in an eternal exchange of love and communion. This call to communion is signified in sexual difference and the call of the two to become one.

Perhaps we could say that, in the Old Testament, the spousal image, when applied to God's love for Israel, reaches only the wedding ceremony, when bridegroom and bride stand in each other's presence confessing their love and commitment. In the New Testament, however, the image also encompasses the wedding night, the consummation in one flesh. In the New Testament, the spousal image "becomes union with God through sharing in Jesus' self-gift, sharing in his body and blood," as Benedict says.

I'd like to ask you to suspend your disbelief for just a moment and walk through the following scenario with me. Imagine that I'm an angel sent by God to give you an important message. You and I are standing before a beautiful stone building. It looks almost like a monument, with a mysterious tower reaching to the heavens. I say to you, "God, the Ultimate Source of the universe, the One, True, Omnipotent, Omniscient, Immutable, Incomprehensible, Infinite, Sovereign, Righteous, Glorious, Holy, Merciful, Loving, Living God who created you, through an incredible self-emptying on his part, has made himself really, truly, actually, substantially *present* in that building." Now, with your disbelief still suspended, imagine it to be true. God, the One Real God, is *really* in there. What would you do? What would you *want* to do?

Imagine I tell you that God will allow you to *enter* that building and *stand in his presence*. What an awesome, unfathomable, glorious opportunity it would be—the chance of a lifetime. But there's more. Suppose I tell you that God will allow you to *see* him through a veil. Inconceivable! But there's more. God will allow you to *reach out and touch him* through that veil. Outrageous!

Let's review: God is actually *in* this building and you are allowed to enter and stand in his presence. You are able to *see* him and *touch* him through a veil. Unfathomable? Inconceivable? Outrageous? All that is *nothing* compared to this final proposition, this final gift. God has told me to tell you—I can barely bring myself to say it. In fact, I asked the Almighty several times in utter bafflement if I had heard him correctly, and he assured me that I had. It's going to sound crazy, preposterous, mad, I know. But again, keep that disbelief suspended. Are you ready? (This is crazy! This is insanely crazy! Deep breath...)—God has told me to tell you that not only does he want you to *be with him* in his presence and to rejoice in *seeing him* and *touching* him, but he wants—in fact, he said it was the deepest yearning of his heart—you to...to *eat him*.

What? Yes, you heard me correctly. *God wants you to consume him—to eat him* so that he can be truly *in* you and *one* with you, and you can be truly *in* him and *one* with him. O taste and see: *taste* and *see* the goodness of the Lord!

The well-known Protestant rebuttal to Catholic faith in Christ's real presence in the Eucharist is not without merit. "You don't *really* believe that is Jesus' body and blood," they say. "If you really believed that was Jesus, you wouldn't walk to communion; you would crawl on your hands and knees to communion." How casual we can be in this most intimate encounter with our God! How obtuse! And yet Christ continues to say, "This is my body given *for you*." He continues to call us. He continues to woo us.

Lord, give us ears to hear your call and a heart to comprehend with all the saints the breadth and length and height and depth of your love, that we may be filled with all the fullness of God poured out in the Eucharist (see Eph 3:18-19).

50. "The sacramental 'mysticism,' grounded in God's condescension towards us, operates at a radically different level and lifts us to far greater heights than anything that any human mystical elevation could ever accomplish" (n. 13).

Men and women of all cultures have sought through various means of meditation, self-discipline, and innumerable other religious practices to encounter the transcendent, to experience "mystical elevation." While these efforts can bear fruit in some limited ways, the human being simply cannot cross that infinite abyss between earth and heaven to grasp God. The only way we can possibly reach the fulfillment for which we long (divine life, immortality) is if God empties himself and crosses that abyss himself, descending from heaven to earth to *reveal* himself to us and *offer* himself to us. We believe that *he has*. It's called the Gospel, the *good news*. It's also called Christianity. No other religion makes the same claims.

In the very first paragraph of the *Catechism of the Catholic Church* we read: "God, infinitely perfect and blessed in himself, in a plan of sheer goodness freely created man to make him [that is, allow him to] share in his own blessed life. For this reason, at every time and in every place, God draws close to man." And "when the fullness of time had come, God sent his Son." There we see God's condescension toward us. But, as the *Catechism* explains, God also "calls man to seek him" (*CCC*, n. I). There we see man's aspiration for God.

Man's searching for God (*eros*) can reach certain levels of elevation, but it can never afford what God's searching for man (*agapē*) can. The two operate at "radically different" levels, as Pope Benedict observes. Still, as we have seen throughout our reflections, there is a profound meeting in God's condescension and our aspirations, our reaching up and his reaching down. There is a profound meeting between *agape* and *eros*, and in this meeting, this embrace of the divine and the human, we experience ecstatic bliss, beatitude—the happiness for which God created us. God does not hoard his glory, as we have already seen. God *is* gift, which is to say, God *is* love.

> 51. "As Saint Paul says, 'Because there is one bread, we who are many are one body, for we all partake of the one bread' (1 Cor 10:17). Union with Christ is also union with all those to whom he gives himself. I cannot possess Christ just for myself; I can belong to him only in union with all those who have become, or who will become, his own" (n. 14).

"It is not good that the man should be alone" (Gen 2:18). In the beginning, in this solitude, Adam discovered his twofold vocation: love of God and love of neighbor. From among all the living creatures of the visible world, Adam alone was called to live in a personal relationship of love and communion with his Creator. Indeed, only the human being had the capacity for such a relationship. But Adam, having been in-spired (in-breathed) with divine love, experienced an explicit need to share that love with another like him. "Therefore a man leaves his father and his mother and clings to his wife, and they become one flesh" (Gen 2:24).

This union in "one body" not only foreshadows Christ's union with the Church. It also foreshadows the union of all the members of the Church who form the "one body" of Christ. In other words, the holy communion of spouses in Genesis is a foreshadowing of the

Holy Communion of the Eucharist. And the Eucharist establishes us not only in union with Christ, but also in union with one another. For, as Pope Benedict expresses it, "Union with Christ is also union with all those to whom he gives himself."

The Eucharist, then, fulfills both dimensions of Adam's original vocation: love of God *and* love of neighbor. At least it is meant to do so. Here on earth we still need to resist and overcome those forces that prevent us from realizing that union in its fullness. In eternity, all will be consummated. All the members of Christ, the communion of saints, will live in the perfect unity of one body. *"For man, this consummation will be the final realization of the unity of the human race, which God willed from creation. ...* Those who are united with Christ will form the community of the redeemed, 'the holy city' of God, 'the Bride, the wife of the Lamb'" (*CCC*, n. 1045). We will know all and be known by all. We will see all and be seen by all. And God will be all in all.

> 52. "Communion draws me out of myself towards him, and thus also towards unity with all Christians. We become 'one body', completely joined in a single existence. Love of God and love of neighbor are now truly united: God incarnate draws us all to himself. We can thus understand how *agape* also became a term for the Eucharist" (n. 14).

As the *Catechism* says, "All men are called to the same end: God himself. There is a certain resemblance between the unity of the divine persons and the fraternity that men are to establish among themselves in truth and love. Love of neighbor is inseparable from love for God" (*CCC*, n. 1878). Elsewhere, the *Catechism* says that the "communion of the Holy Trinity is the source and criterion of truth in every relationship. It is lived out in prayer, above all in the Eucharist" (*CCC*, n. 2845).

What remarkable statements! The unity of men and women— not just in marriage but in all human relationships, from the local to the global level—is meant to resemble the unity found in the Trinity. In fact, the communion of the Holy Trinity is the model and measure of truth in *all* human relationships, so the Christian faith professes. Human beings are created to live as the Holy Trinity lives: in a life of happiness and bliss; a life of ever-exchanging love; a life of perfect unity that does not blur the beautiful distinction of each person. Is this merely a pipe dream? Is this merely pie-in-the-sky idealism? It is true that, here on earth, life will always fall short of what it is meant to be. Christian hope is not utopian. We are pilgrims awaiting our true home in eternity. That being said, God has already made true love and communion a possibility even here on earth in the death and resurrection of Jesus.

In Christ, we "become 'one body,' completely joined in a single existence," as Benedict says. But just as the three Persons in God retain their own identities, this deep organic unity does not cancel out our individuality. Rather, it perfects it and makes it shine forth in all its brilliance. To use the technical language of John Paul II, the human race is destined to live in a *"perfect intersubjectivity of all"* (*TOB* 68:4) that "will not absorb man's personal subjectivity, but, quite on the contrary, will make it emerge in an incomparably greater and fuller measure" (*TOB* 67:3). To speak of "subjectivity" here means to speak of the mystery of the human person in all its interior depth.

The human being is not merely an "object" in the world; he is a *subject*, a self-determining agent with inalienable dignity. As subjects, as persons, we are called to use our self-determination to enter into loving relationship with others. We are called to live in communion with other persons, or, as John Paul II said, we are called to "inter-subjectivity." In this way we come to realize "the 'trinitarian order' in the created world of persons" (*TOB* 68:4).

But when we focus on the human subject without recognizing his call to communion with others, we end with "individualism" or "subjectivism" rather than "inter-subjectivity." Such is the case when we cut off *eros* from *agape*. Erotic love cut off from divine love is not interested in the sacrifices required of living in communion with others. Left to itself, as we have already observed, *eros* is interested only in its own subjective pleasure. It is *agape*, poured out in the Eucharist, that "draws me out of myself," says Benedict. It is *agape*, revealed and poured out superabundantly *in Christ's body*, that draws us out of ourselves because "God incarnate draws us all to himself." When we behold God incarnate, when we behold the divine mystery of love revealed through his body (theology of the body), we are drawn to the beauty that is our very life, our very reason for existence, the satisfaction of every last longing and desire. "I, when I am lifted up from the earth, will draw all men to myself" (Jn 12:32).

53. In "the Eucharist...God's own *agape* comes to us bodily" (n. 14).

How can this be? How can God, who is pure Spirit, communicate his sacrificial *agape* love to us *bodily*? He can do so in Jesus Christ, for "in him the whole fullness of deity dwells bodily" (Col 2:9). Outrageous! Yes, Christianity *is* outrageous. It claims that God "has made himself visible in the flesh" (*CCC*, n. 1159). It claims that the "'flesh is the hinge of salvation.' We believe in God who is creator of the flesh; we believe in the Word made flesh in order to redeem the flesh; we believe in the resurrection of the flesh, the fulfillment of both the creation and the redemption of the flesh" (*CCC*, n. 1015). Praise be to God for flesh, for human flesh, for male and female flesh, and for the two becoming one flesh!

If this strikes anyone as an "un-Christian" prayer, it's because we have been influenced by un-Christian, dualistic ideas about the relationship of flesh and spirit. Angelo Cardinal Scola, Patriarch of Venice, observes that, from the authentic Christian perspective, the human person "can never be considered in dualistic terms. There can never be a separation or opposition between spirit and body, whether direct or indirect." A disincarnate spirituality is rooted in a false split between body and soul. From this perspective, the "body is understood as…a prison that prevents the soul from fully being itself. Such a perspective," Scola concludes, "challenges the very essence of Christianity" (*NM*, pp. 260, 262).

For the essence of Christianity is Word made flesh—spirit and matter united in an embrace of love that will never end. The essence of Christianity is that "God's own *agape* comes to us bodily": "This is my body which is given for you" (Lk 22:19).

Jesus, grant us the faith to believe in so great a gift and to receive it with praise and gratitude!

54. "Faith, worship, and *ethos* are interwoven as a single reality which takes shape in our encounter with God's *agape*. Here the usual contraposition between worship and ethics simply falls apart. 'Worship' itself, Eucharistic communion, includes the reality both of being loved and of loving others in turn. A Eucharist which does not pass over into the concrete practice of love is intrinsically fragmented" (n. 14).

If *faith* is the openness of the human heart to God's gift, *worship* is the gratitude we express to God for so great a gift, and *ethos* is our yearning to be the same gift to others that God is to us. These three realities—faith, worship, and ethos—"are interwoven as a single reality." But this single reality "takes shape" only "in our encounter with God's *agape*."

"Encounter" is a key word here. When a person *encounters* divine love, he meets the foundation of his very being, the reality from which and for which he is created. The fallen world's repeated lessons that authentic love is not real, that love does not exist or is not possible, give way to faith as the heart opens up to receive so great a gift: a share in the Trinity's own fire, a share in the Trinity's own mystery of eternal love-generation. Love of God (worship) and love of neighbor (ethos) flow naturally and readily from the presence of that fire within the human heart.

Worship, Pope Benedict tells us, includes both the reality of being loved and of loving others. But for the creature, being loved *always* precedes the reality of loving others. "We love, because he first loved us" (1 Jn 4:19). Only to the degree that we know we are loved are we able to love others. As we mentioned earlier, one cannot give what he does not have. Failure in loving others stems from not living in God's love for us. Hence, when we fail to meet the moral norm calling us to love, what we need is not more willpower. Nor do we need someone shoving the law down our throats. Rather, what we need is a deeper "encounter" with divine love. In this encounter, and only in this encounter, does "ethic"—the law, the external moral norm—become "ethos," a deep yearning and power from within to fulfill the law by being the same gift to others that God is to us. Instead of *having* to love, we *want* to love.

In God's love for us, the Father, through the Son, shares with us his own "love-gift," which is the Holy Spirit. Filled with this fire, we long to return it to God (worship) and share it with others (ethos). When we step out of that circuit of love, we short-circuit. We still long for love but seek it in the wrong places. Consequently, despite all intentions to the contrary, we fail to love others rightly when we are unplugged from the source.

The Eucharist is the sure means for "plugging ourselves in" to that electricity, that fire of love. In the Mass, the Bride receives the gift of the heavenly Bridegroom, who "impregnates" her with fire and then sends her forth on a mission (*missio*, from which we derive "Mass") to bear that fire to others. If we have opened our hearts to that fire, our mission to "Go in peace to love and serve the Lord" becomes our heart's deepest desire.

How do we "love and serve the Lord"? The apostle John tells us: "For this is the love of God, that we keep his commandments. And his commandments are not burdensome" (I Jn 5:3). They aren't? No, they aren't if we are ablaze with the fire of his love. Only when we step away from that "circuit" of Trinitarian love-fire do we find it difficult and even impossible to keep God's commandments. If we find God's commandments burdensome, perhaps the solution is not to reject the commandments or water them down. Perhaps the solution is to step into the fire, to be set ablaze with love, to be reborn in that divine mystery of love-generation. "For whatever is born of God overcomes the world; and this is the victory that overcomes the world, our faith" (I Jn 5:4).

Faith opens to fire, *worship* returns the fire to God, and *ethos* shares the fire with others. All three "are interwoven as a single reality." That single reality is an eternal blazing fire, which has become "real food" and "real drink" (see Jn 6:55).

55. "No one has ever seen God as he is. And yet God is not totally invisible to us...God has made himself visible: in Jesus we are able to see the Father (cf. Jn 14:9)" (n. 17).

What enables us to "see the Father"? At the risk of sounding like a broken record, we must turn once again to the inexhaustible mystery of the Incarnation. In the fullness of time, God sent his son, born of a woman. In Christ's human body, God's mystery becomes visible. This is why John Paul II spoke of the body as a *theology*. In the thesis statement of his famous teaching, John Paul stated that the "body, in fact, and only the body, is capable of making visible what is invisible: the spiritual and the divine. It has been created to transfer into the visible reality of the world, the mystery hidden from eternity in God, and thus to be a sign of it" (*TOB* 19:4). That's an impressive assertion, but what does it mean?

We cannot see spiritual realities. By definition, they are invisible. But the human body is capable of making invisible realities visible so that we can see and touch them. Because of the Incarnation, the apostles can proclaim that the word of life "which we have seen with our eyes, which we have looked upon and touched with our hands... was made manifest, and we saw it, and testify to it" (I Jn I:I-2). The *Catechism* observes that God "impressed his own form on the flesh... in such a way that even what was visible might bear the divine form" (*CCC*, n. 704).

What is the divine form? "God himself is an eternal exchange of love, Father, Son, and Holy Spirit" (*CCC*, n. 221). God impressed this Trinitarian form right in our flesh by creating us as male and female and calling us to be fruitful and multiply. In the union and fertility of the sexes, we discover a "created version" of the Trinity's Uncreated "exchange of love." Of course, we must always remember the abyss that exists between the created and the Uncreated. This created communion (male-female) provides only a faint glimmer, only a pale image of the Uncreated Communion (the Trinity). But it does provide an image nonetheless. As John Paul II affirmed in a dramatic development of Catholic thought, man images God "not only through his own humanity, but also through the communion of persons which man and woman form right from the beginning." He even said that this "constitutes, perhaps, the deepest theological aspect of everything one can say about man" (*TOB* 9:3).

Since Christ is the perfect image of God in the world, we are more accurately images of *the* Image. We are images of Christ in his incarnate union with the Church. Those who see others purely see Jesus in his union with the Church. And, as Benedict says, "in Jesus we are able to see the Father."

Chapter 9

THE JOURNEY OF LOVE

56. When God commands us to love, he "does not demand of us a feeling which we ourselves are incapable of producing. He loves us, he makes us see and experience his love, and since he has 'loved us first,' love can also blossom as a response within us" (n. 17).

We are called to love as God loves. This, however, poses a fundamental problem. Divine love (*agape*) is just that—*divine*. It does not originate in us. But God himself has offered us the opportunity to participate in his own nature, to participate in his divine fire, to share in his own eternal, ecstatic exchange of love. To the degree that we allow this divine gift to penetrate and permeate us, "love can also blossom as a response within us," as the Holy Father expresses.

In chapter one we observed that "holiness is measured according to the 'great mystery' in which the Bride responds with the gift of love to the gift of the Bridegroom" (*CCC*, n. 773). The key for understanding this mystery is Mary. "Mary goes before us all in the holiness that is the Church's mystery as 'the bride without spot or wrinkle.' This is why the 'Marian' dimension of the Church precedes the 'Petrine'" (*CCC*, n. 773).

This passage is filled with riches that can help us understand the above quotation from Pope Benedict. The Church is both of Mary and of Peter. The "Marian" dimension of the Church refers to the Church's contemplative mystery as a Bride who, in her very being, is invited to *open* and *receive* the gift of the Bridegroom. Only in receiving does the Church "bear divine life" within. The "Petrine" dimension of the Church refers to the Church's apostolic activity, her mission to proclaim Christ to the world "in re-membrance" of him. But the Church can only give what she herself has first received (she cannot "member" Christ, only "re-member" him). Hence, the Marian dimension always precedes the Petrine; the receiving always comes before the going out. If it did not, the Church would not be proclaiming Christ but something of her own invention, something merely human.

This applies in its own way to each and every believer. We must be contemplative before we are active. We must receive before we give. We must be filled up before we can pour out. If we do not, we will find the love God calls us to impossible, and we will inevitably settle for a love of our own invention. Without a "Marian" perspective in love—opening first to receive God's love—*eros* is effectively cut off from *agape*. Mary, then, is the one who shows us the true meaning of *eros!* True *eros* is always open to the penetration and permeation of the divine. Indeed, the true purpose of *eros* is to open us to the divine. This is why Mary goes before us all on the journey of learning to love.

57. "Love is not merely a sentiment. Sentiments come and go. A sentiment can be a marvelous first spark, but it is not the fullness of love" (n. 17).

Sentiments and attractions are fickle. They often disappear as quickly as they appear, and one might experience them toward any number of people. Should I confess to my wife, "I'm in love with another woman," because I experienced a stirring of emotion toward this "other woman" or found her attractive? The nonsensicalness of such a notion demonstrates just how shallow "love" is when we reduce it to mere sentiment. "A sentiment can be a marvelous first spark," as the Holy Father observes, but it most certainly "is not the fullness of love."

Bishop Karol Wojtyla, long before becoming Pope John Paul II, offered a piercing analysis of this truth in his book *Love and Responsibility*. He describes the rousing of sentiment and attraction as the "raw material" of love but warned that we must never mistake it for love's "finished form" (see *LR*, p. 139). Such "raw material" *can* furnish the opportunity for love to grow and mature. But sentiments and attractions must be "held together by the correct gravitational pull," as Wojtyla put it. If they are not, they "may add up not to love, but to its direct opposite." For oftentimes what we call "love," if we take a deeper look, "turns out to be, contrary to all appearances, only a form of 'utilization' of the person" (*LR*, p. 146, 167).

The "correct gravitational pull" that enables sentiment and attraction to become love is the value of the person *as a person*. When "love" is based merely on attraction and sentiment, the decisive feature of the relationship is not the good *of the other* as a person, but the pleasure of the sentiment and sensual reactions that the other person stirs *in me*. When the pleasure dissipates, which it inevitably does, so does the "love."

In such a relationship, as Wojtyla writes, "one person belongs to another as an object of use, and tries to derive some pleasure from allowing that other to make use of him or her. Such an attitude, on both sides, is utterly incompatible with love." Such an attitude, in fact, amounts to little more than egoism. And building a relationship on egoism is like building a house on sand. "The ricketyness of the structure must show itself in time. It is one of the greatest of sorrows when love proves to be not what it was thought to be, but its diagonal opposite" (*LR*, p. 128).

Does the fickleness of our sentiments and attractions and the danger of confusing them with love mean that it is our duty to distrust the human heart? John Paul II answers emphatically, "No! It is only to say that we must remain in control of it" (*TOB* 32:3). In other words, we must learn how to direct the reactions of our hearts toward the true dignity of the person. We must follow Christ the whole way to Calvary, allowing him to "crucify" the consumer orientation of *eros*, infusing it, instead, with his own sacrificial *agape*. This is a life-long process of purification and maturation, as Pope Benedict says in the following passage.

58. "The process of purification and maturation by which *eros* comes fully into its own…is always open-ended; love is never 'finished' and complete; throughout life, it changes and matures, and thus remains faithful to itself" (n. 17).

How easily, at times, the words "I love you" roll off my tongue toward my wife, Wendy. Yes, it's true; I *do* love her. However, it would be more accurate for me to say, "I am learning to love you" or "I am growing in my love for you." For love, as Pope Benedict wisely observes, "is never 'finished' and complete; throughout life it changes and matures." Karol Wojtyla put it this way, "Love should be seen as something which in a sense never 'is' but is always only 'becoming,' and what it becomes depends upon the contribution of both persons and the depth of their commitment" (*LR*, n. 139).

Allow me to share how this truth has been a hard-learned lesson (and one I am still learning!) in my own life. During my late teen years, I was involved in a long-term dating relationship fraught with all the tensions, difficulties, and wounds that come when people confuse lust with love. In my early twenties, I began a quest to understand why God made us male and female in the first place and what this whole "sex thing" was about. Discovering John Paul II's extensive teaching on human love and sexuality was like a balm placed on my open wounds. I began healing—key word, *began*.

When I started dating my wife, Wendy, things were *radically* different in comparison with my "lustful days." I had never experienced anything like it. I *saw* her value as a person and wanted nothing more than to uphold it. I wasn't bound to indulge my lustful impulses as I had been before. *Eros* was being liberated by *agape*. I could *feel* it. I was totally convinced that this was it—this was love! And it was. But it was love that was *only beginning*, only *coming into being*. In many ways, because I had journeyed so far, I mistakenly thought I had already "arrived." Intellectually I knew and accepted that love grows and matures, but I had no idea how many mountains I still had left to climb. I was too elated at having reached the top of what, it turns out, was only the first peak in a vast range. There I was, jumping up and down like Rocky Balboa with arms raised high: "Yo, Wendy, I did it! I learned how to love!" Or so I thought. Mercy, Jesus.

Because of the work I do, many people view me as an "authority" on God's plan for man and woman. How easy it would be for me to succumb to the illusion—since I'm the "expert"—that I've already figured out this whole love-sex-marriage thing. Allow me to take a page out of St. Paul's book. In his second letter to the Corinthians, Paul boasts of his accomplishments, not only to demonstrate how ridiculous such boasting is but also to demonstrate that, in reality, all we have going for us is our weaknesses (see 2 Cor 11-12). Like Paul, I am out of my mind to say such things, but here goes: I'm Christopher West. I'm the guy who has devoted his life to studying and teaching the Theology of the Body. I've immersed myself in it. I know the contents of John Paul II's teaching backward and forward, inside and out. I've been to every lecture I've ever given, attended every course I've ever taught, and read every book and article I've ever written...and, oh, how painful a lesson it has been to realize that giving lectures, teaching courses, and writing books and articles *about* God's plan for marital love is one thing; *living it* is another.

So, "if I must boast, I will boast of the things that show my weakness" (2 Cor 11:30). Truth be told, in my married life, I have been a lot like the apostle Peter before Pentecost: full of zeal but unable to follow through on countless occasions; quick to jump out of the boat, and quick to sink. Praise God for his mercy and for my dear wife's. Learning to love is a journey and, at times, a very difficult one. But, let us take consolation in the Lord's words to St. Paul: "My grace is sufficient for you, for my power is made perfect in weakness" (2 Cor 12:9). As Karol Wojtyla expressed it, "There is no need to be dismayed if love sometimes follows tortuous ways. Grace has the power to make straight the paths of human love" (*LR*, n. 140).

> 59. "To want the same thing, and to reject the same thing—[this] was recognized by antiquity as the authentic content of love: the one becomes similar to the other, and this leads to a community of will and thought. The love-story between God and man consists in the very fact that this communion of will increases in a communion of thought and sentiment, and thus our will and God's will increasingly coincide: God's will is no longer for me an alien will, something imposed on me from without by the commandments, but it is now my own will" (n. 17).

How many people do you know—maybe it's even true of yourself—who consider Christianity nothing but a long list of oppressive rules to follow, especially when it comes to sex and marital love? Jesus Christ did not die on a cross and rise from the dead to give us a long list of rules to follow! He came to reconcile us in the "love-story between God and man." To the degree that we enter this love story, we come to realize that Christ's mission is not to impose a bunch of rules on us. On the contrary, Christ's mission is to *set us free from the rules*. Let me explain.

As St. Paul tells us, if we are led by the Holy Spirit, we are free from the law (see Gal 5:18). But this doesn't mean we are free to break the law. Christ sets us free to *fulfill* the law. "Do not think that I have come to abolish the law and the prophets; I have come not to abolish them but to fulfil them" (Mt 5:17). Christ fulfills the law, as the word implies, by living it to the full. This means not only meeting the law's demands externally, but living them to the full internally, from the depths of the heart. *Eros-agape* love needs no law, for it *is* the law of life, *even life eternal*.

We all know that it's possible to follow the rules without ever growing in holiness. It's called "legalism" or "moralism." It leads to hypocrisy. "You blind Pharisee! first cleanse the inside of the cup and of the plate, that the outside also may be clean" (Mt 23:26). This is what the grace of the Gospel affords: it presents us not only with a law to follow but with *the power* (God's grace) to fulfill it. Christ didn't come into the world to shove laws down our rebellious throats. He came into the world to change our hearts so that we would no longer need the laws. As the *Catechism* says, "The Law of the Gospel...does not add new external precepts, but proceeds to reform the heart, the root of human acts, where man chooses between the pure and the impure" (*CCC*, n. 1968).

This doesn't mean laws serve no purpose for us. To the degree that our hearts are still rebelling against God's will, we need his law to tell us where our hearts need to change. But if we welcome

God's grace in our lives and allow it to work in us, we come, as Benedict says, to experience with God "a communion of thought and sentiment, and thus our will and God's will increasingly coincide." To the extent that we reject what God rejects and want what he wants, we are "free from the law." Again, this doesn't mean we are free to break the law. We are free to fulfill the law because we no longer desire to break it.

To demonstrate this point in my lectures, I usually call on a married man and ask him if he has any desire to murder his wife. So far (thank God), I've gotten the answer I expect: an emphatic no. Then I'll ask him if he needs the commandment "Thou shalt not murder thy wife." He realizes, of course, that he does not. In this case, the husband is free from the law: not free to break it, but free to fulfill it because he does not desire to break it. To draw the point out further, I'll then call on his wife and ask her if she has ever seen her husband slamming his fists, exclaiming, "Why do those old celibate men in Rome tell me I can't murder my wife? What do they know about marriage, anyway?" The audience laughs, heads nod, and they begin to get my point: we are bitter toward the law only when we desire to break it.

Pick any teaching of the Church that you are bitter about. Chances are it has something to do with sex (we're not usually bitter about the fact that the Church calls us to feed the hungry). Here's a proposal to chew on. Maybe the problem is not with the teaching of the Church. Maybe, just maybe, the problem is precisely what Jesus said it was: our own hardness of heart (see Mt 19:8). And maybe the solution is not to throw the Church's teaching out the window.

Maybe the solution, instead, is to get on our knees and humbly pray, "Lord, please change my heart."

> **60. "Love of neighbor…consists in the very fact that, in God and with God, I love even the person whom I do not like or even know. This can only take place on the basis of an intimate encounter with God, an encounter which has become a communion of will, even affecting my feelings"** (n. 18).

Love your enemies? Most of us have a hard enough time loving our friends. How can we love our enemies? How can I love the guy who cut me off in traffic? How can I love that coworker who stabbed me in the back and took the promotion that *I* deserve? How can I love my husband who physically and verbally abused me and ran off with another woman? How can I love the person whom I do not like or even know? Pope Benedict gives us the answer: "This can only take place on the basis of an intimate encounter with God." Only "in God and with God" can I love my enemies and do good to those who harm me. This love does not originate in human hearts. It is a divine love that can, if we allow it, operate within us and through us.

The more we allow God's love to move in us, the more we experience "a communion of will" with God, a communion that even affects our feelings. In fact, as the *Catechism* teaches, "moral perfection consists in man's being moved to the good not by his will alone, but also by his sensitive appetite, as in the words of the psalm: 'My heart and flesh sing for joy to the living God'" (*CCC*, n. 1770). The fullness of Christian life does not consist merely in submitting one's rebellious heart to God's commandments by force of will. That's an essential first stage on the journey towards the perfection of love, but it is an essentially purgative stage. In what the great saints have called the "unitive stage" of the spiritual journey, the Christian has progressed from merely avoiding sin by force of will to living in such deep union with Jesus that he is able to love with Jesus' own heart.

Intense prayer is the path to this new heart. As John Paul II taught us in a marvelous passage from his letter on the new millennium, "Prayer can progress, as a genuine dialogue of love, to the point of rendering the person wholly possessed by the divine Beloved, vibrating at the Spirit's touch, resting filially within the Father's heart." To be wholly possessed by the God who *is* love enables our hearts to love not only *as* he loves but *with his love*. This, John Paul continued, "is a journey totally sustained by grace, which nonetheless demands an intense spiritual commitment and is no stranger to painful purifications (the 'dark night'). But it leads, in various possible ways, to the ineffable joy experienced by the mystics as 'nuptial union'" (*NMI*, n. 33). This, as we have said many times throughout this book, is the divine plan for us all: God wants to "marry" us, to unite with us in the flesh—in-carnation—and thus assume us into His own eternal exchange of ecstatic life-giving love.

It is through prayer that we experience this divine-human "nuptial union." John Paul II implores us: "Yes, dear brothers and sisters, our Christian communities must become *genuine 'schools' of prayer*...until the heart truly 'falls in love'...By opening our heart to the love of God [intense prayer] also opens it to the love of our brothers and sisters" (*NMI*, n. 33). The more we experience that divine love-fire burning in us, the more we yearn to share that love with others. Indeed, we find ourselves overcome with love for those we do not like or even know. In these experiences of love, we can truly say with St. Paul that "it is no longer I who live, but Christ who lives in me" (Gal 2:20). It is no longer I who love, but Christ who loves in me.

> **61. As I grow in love, "I learn to look on this other person not simply with my eyes and with my feelings, but from the perspective of Jesus Christ....Going beyond exterior appearances, I perceive in others an interior desire for a sign of love, of concern....Seeing with the eyes of Christ, I can give to others...the look of love which they crave" (n. 18).**

I'd like to reflect on this quotation by sharing another personal experience. Not long ago, as I was walking through an airport terminal, I saw a young, attractive woman who was rather scantily clad. As I passed her, I looked her in the eye, hoping that, amidst the numerous lustful gazes I'm sure she received, she would somehow sense that I wanted to honor her and uphold her dignity. I wished I had the opportunity to sit down with her and tell her how much God loved her and to share with her the true goodness and dignity of her femininity.

Well, what do you know? This very person happened to be on my flight. And who would have guessed? Her ticket landed her right next to me on the plane. *This is going to be an interesting flight*, I thought. I was certain I knew what God was up to. Little did I know.

As I was running various options through my head as to how I might start a conversation with her, another woman sat to my left. To put it frankly, she was not a picture of what the world would consider feminine beauty. In fact, her choice of clothes and her butch haircut made her look a lot like the stereotypical "lesbian." We struck up a friendly conversation, during which she casually told me that she was flying to meet her "partner" to look at a new house that they planned to buy. *Wow, Lord,* I thought. *What's going on here? I have a scantily clad beauty to my right and a masculinely clad "lesbian" to my left. Help me, Lord, to love them both as you do,* I prayed.

My natural tendency was to favor conversation with the "beautiful" woman, but, as it turned out, I never said a word to her. Instead, I continued chitchatting with Helen (not her real name), the woman to my left. We talked about any number of things. We joked a bit and laughed together. I imagined she'd eventually ask me what I do for a living, and I'd have an open door to introduce her to John Paul II's beautiful vision of human love. But it never came up. Instead of teaching her *about* God's love, it seems God wanted me to *show* her his love. He wanted her in some way to *experience* it through me. I was to be a little glimpse of his love for her in the flesh. And he also wanted to teach *me* a valuable lesson.

At one point during the flight, both women fell asleep. As I sat between them, I imagined the lives they'd both lived and the wounds they'd most likely endured at the hands of men. I knew that each woman, in her own way, was actually looking for the love that Jesus gives. *Help me to show it to them, Lord. Help them to know that, despite my fallen humanity, I am a man who wants to love them both rightly.* Then an image came to mind, almost as if I were dreaming. A sword pierced my heart, revealing its true contents. At first, glops of brown sludge spewed out. This, I think, represented my fallen humanity, my tendency to want to use the "beautiful" woman for my own pleasure and my tendency to want to discard the "less than beautiful" woman because she was of "no value" to me. *Lord, I see my sinfulness. Please redeem me! Please cleanse me! Please give me your love for them!* As I offered that prayer, the sludge slowly turned to a cleaner trickle of water, then to a steady flow, and then to a fountain of pure water gushing out of my heart in two directions—toward the woman on my right and toward the woman on my left—and seeming to bathe the two in love. It was unlike anything I had ever experienced.

Later, as the plane landed, Helen and I exchanged sincere goodbyes: "You're a swell guy, Christopher. I sure enjoyed talking with you." "Well, you're a swell gal, Helen, and I really enjoyed talking with you, too." I meant it. In fact, as I said it, a lump formed in my throat. I was overflowing with an unexpected holy love for this woman. Helen was a few steps ahead of me as we exited the jetway. As she turned to walk down the terminal, I said one more time, "See ya, Helen." All the hustle and bustle of the terminal seemed suspended for a moment as she turned around and caught my eye. Love was pouring out of me, and I knew she felt it. With a sense of surprise and a delighted smile she said, "See ya, Christopher."

As she walked away, it was all I could do to hold back the tears. *Jesus, Jesus, I want to be in heaven with that person. I want to rejoice with her forever in your love. Please, Lord, see her safely home to heaven. See her safely through her trials and one day reunite us in your eternal love. Please, Jesus, I want to live with her forever.* Right then my cell phone rang. It was my wife. When I answered, I couldn't even talk. "What is it? What's wrong?" she asked. "Wendy," I stammered through my tears, "I know this sounds strange, but I just fell in love with a 'lesbian.'" My tears turned to chuckles of delight as I realized how crazy that would sound to the world.

On a side note, I put the term "lesbian" in quotes because I refuse to define anyone with such a term. Helen is just a woman who, like everyone else, is looking for love. Sadly, like so many of us, she has looked for it in the wrong places, which is all the more reason to seek to love her rightly. I know Helen experienced love that day. And I know it was not I who was loving her, but Jesus in me. Later, as I reflected on the experience, I remembered the above words of Pope Benedict: As we grow in love, Jesus takes us "beyond exterior appearances." Seeing with the eyes of Jesus, we "can give to others. . .the look of love which they crave."

62. If I live "solely out of a desire to be 'devout' and to perform my 'religious duties', then my relationship with God. . .becomes merely 'proper,' but loveless" (n. 18).

And what is a devout and dutiful but loveless religiosity worth? What is a "proper" but loveless relationship with God worth? St. Paul provides a stark answer: "If I speak in the tongues of men and of angels, but have not love, I am a noisy gong or a clanging cymbal. And if I have prophetic powers, and understand all mysteries and all knowledge, and if I have all faith, so as to move mountains, but have not love, I am nothing. If I give away all I have, and if I deliver my body to be burned, but have not love, I gain nothing" (I Cor 13:1-3).

The converse of the apostle Paul's "nothing" is to say that love is *everything*. The purpose of religious devotion is to grow more deeply in God's love for us and, in turn, to express our love for God and neighbor. To recite rote prayers in a loveless way or to go to church on Sunday merely to punch one's attendance card is virtually meaningless. I say "virtually" meaningless because it is certainly true that God's love can always break through a person's "loveless religiosity" and, indeed, religious practices themselves can dispose us to such a breakthrough. But, in the final analysis, if I go to Mass every day and do not grow in love, I gain nothing. If I give large sums of money to the poor but have not love, I am nothing. If I mentally accept all the Church's teachings and have not love, I gain nothing.

In fact, religion without love—just like sex without love—turns man against himself and becomes a terribly destructive phenomenon. History offers no shortage of examples of the destruction that religious conviction wreaks when it is cut off from the truth that God is love. "In a world where the name of God is sometimes associated with vengeance or even a duty of hatred and violence, this message," Pope Benedict tells us, "is both timely and significant. For this reason, I wish in my first Encyclical to speak of the love which God lavishes upon us and which we in turn must share with others" (n. I).

63. "Love grows through love. Love is 'divine' because it comes from God and unites us to God; through this

unifying process it makes us a 'we' which transcends our divisions and makes us one, until in the end God is 'all in all' (1 Cor 15:28)" (n. 18).

This final quotation provides a fitting opportunity to summarize these reflections. Throughout we have been pondering the truth that God is love. At the foundation of all that is, we find not some divine clock maker, not some impersonal force, not a tyrant with a will to lord it over us. We find an eternal exchange of love: Father, Son, and Holy Spirit. We find a God who longs to share his own goodness, love, and bliss with his creatures, with man. How can we plumb the depths of such a mystery, of such a gift? In his mercy, God has "transcribed" his own divine mystery in human language, making it accessible to us. Indeed, it is very close to us. For God inscribed a sign of his own mystery, of his own divine "We" right in our humanity by creating us male and female and calling us to a human "we."

"Then God said, 'Let us make man in our image, after our likeness...' So God created man in his own image, in the image of God he created him; male and female he created them. And God blessed them, and God said to them, 'Be fruitful and multiply.'" (Gen 1:26-28). From the beginning, God calls man and woman to fulfill the divine image through their love for each other: "Therefore a man leaves his father and his mother and clings to his wife, and they become one flesh" (Gen 2:24). As we have learned, from the beginning of creation, *eros* was meant to express *agape*—that is, human, erotic love was meant to express divine, sacrificial love. Indeed, the joining of spouses as "one"—with all its blood, sweat, tears, and joys—was meant to be a sign in the world that communicated God's eternal plan for the cosmos: that all things would be united as "one" in Christ Jesus (see Eph 1:9-10). As the author of the letter to the Ephesians proclaims, the union of spouses in one flesh is "a great mystery," and it refers to Christ and his union with the Church (see 5:31-32).

The love, then, of man and woman (*eros*) establishes itself and grows through the love God lavishes on us (*agape*). As Benedict says, "Love grows through love. Love is 'divine' because it comes from God and unites us to God; through this unifying process it makes us a 'we' which transcends our divisions and makes us one." But what would happen if love were cut off from love—that is, if *eros* were cut off from *agape*? As Pope Benedict says, *eros* removed from *agape* "is not an ascent in 'ecstasy' towards the Divine, but a fall, a degradation of man. Evidently, *eros* needs to be disciplined and purified if it is to provide not just fleeting pleasure, but a certain foretaste of the pinnacle of our existence, of that beatitude for which our whole being yearns" (n. 4).

But how can *eros* be disciplined and purified so that it leads us to the happiness for which we yearn? Is such love even possible? In light of human frailty and weakness, it would seem that the love to which we are called simply does not correspond to man's concrete possibilities. John Paul II once responded to just such an objection with what may well be one of the boldest proclamations of the power of the Gospel in the Church's history: "What are the 'concrete possibilities of man'?" he asked. "And of *which* man are we speaking? Of man *dominated* by lust or of man *redeemed by Christ*? This is what is at stake: the *reality* of Christ's redemption. *Christ has redeemed us!* This means that he has given us the possibility of realizing the *entire* truth of our being; he has set our freedom free from the *domination* of concupiscence. And if redeemed man still sins, this is not due to an imperfection of Christ's redemptive act, but to man's will not to avail himself of the grace which flows from that act." God's call to love as he loves "is of course proportioned to man's capabilities; but to the capabilities of the man to whom the Holy Spirit has been given" (*VS*, n. 103).

This is the good news of the Gospel: "God's love has been poured into our hearts through the Holy Spirit who has been given to us" (Rom 5:5). The men and women who welcome this glorious gift discover *the love that satisfies.*

Come Holy Spirit.

Come fill our hearts with the fire of your love,

so that we might set the world ablaze!

INDEX

About the Author

Christopher West is recognized around the world for his work promoting an integral, biblical vision of human life, love, and sexuality. He serves as a research fellow and faculty member of the Theology of the Body Institute near Philadelphia. He has also lectured on a number of other prestigious faculties, offering graduate and undergraduate courses at St John Vianney Seminary in Denver, the John Paul II Institute in Melbourne, Australia, and the Institute for Priestly Formation at Creighton University in Omaha.

In addition, Christopher is the best selling author of four books and one of the most sought-after speakers in the Church today, having delivered more than 1,000 public lectures on four continents, in ten countries, and in nearly 200 American cities. His popular column "Body Language" is syndicated to diocesan newspapers around the country. Christopher and his wife, Wendy, live with their four children near Lancaster, Pennsylvania.